JERSEY CITY WESTBOUND

By JOHN HENDERSON

H&M PRODUCTIONS
193-07 45th Avenue
Flushing, NY 11358

All photographs by the author except where otherwise noted.

ALL RIGHTS RESERVED. This book may not be reproduced, stored in a retrieval system, or transmitted in any form by either electronic or by photo reproduction without written permission from the publisher.

INTRODUCTION

Most people tend to view the years of their young adulthood as special years and railfans are no exception. Every buff thinks his years were the best for photography. In spite of this, when I look at the overall history of railroads and the development of cameras and film, I truly believe that my years, the nineteen fifties and sixties, were the golden years for being a railfan. The variety of motive power, steam, diesel and electric, we had to photograph caused us consternation. When we had a beautiful day we didn't know where to go first. The kaleidoscope of color schemes just screamed photograph me. The hustle and bustle of many and varied terminals dispatching a plethora of limiteds to a myriad of farflung destinations gave the railfan the feeling of being a witness to matters of great moment. This motivated us to brave heat and cold, for we felt a social duty to record these matters of moment for future generations.

The Central Railroad of New Jersey was always a favorite railroad of mine. Its operation was easier to capture on film than big roads like the Penn. and the Central, yet it was not so small that it lacked photographic variety. It was possible in the time of a normal length slide show to encompass the total operation. The supply of equipment meant that no two slides had to have identical subject matter. This, combined with the fact that part of its operation was about to disappear, gave me the right amount of impetus to go out and cover Jersey City before the final curtain.

For the ease of the reader, I have prepared each photo caption so that it stands alone, but can be read from first to last as a continuous text with pictures.

I must thank Henry Maywald who inspired me to put this photo essay together and who aided me every step of the way through the publishing process. I must also thank William J. Brennan, photographer extraordinnaire, for his photographic contribution. Bill was my constant companion in those golden years and a great person to walk the tracks of life with.

DEDICATION

To Elmer "Tiger" Tyukodi, recently deceased, and my buddy for almost forty years — a finer friend is hard to find.

The diesel powered (no, there is no camelback on the head end of this train) 5:02 PM Pt. Pleasant train departs the terminal in a scene reminiscent of the days when steam ruled the Jersey Central.

All photographs by the author except where otherwise noted.

ALL RIGHTS RESERVED. This book may not be reproduced, stored in a retrieval system, or transmitted in any form by either electronic or by photo reproduction without written permission from the publisher.

ALDENE PLAN
Commuter Report

   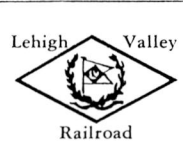 

Issued by the New Jersey Department of Transportation

This is the cover of a brochure distributed to commuters explaining the changes that were to occur. Much was to be abandoned in order to improve, or so said the railroad companies and the State of New Jersey. Less is more is a favorite advertising ploy when change, i.e. reductions, are about to take place.

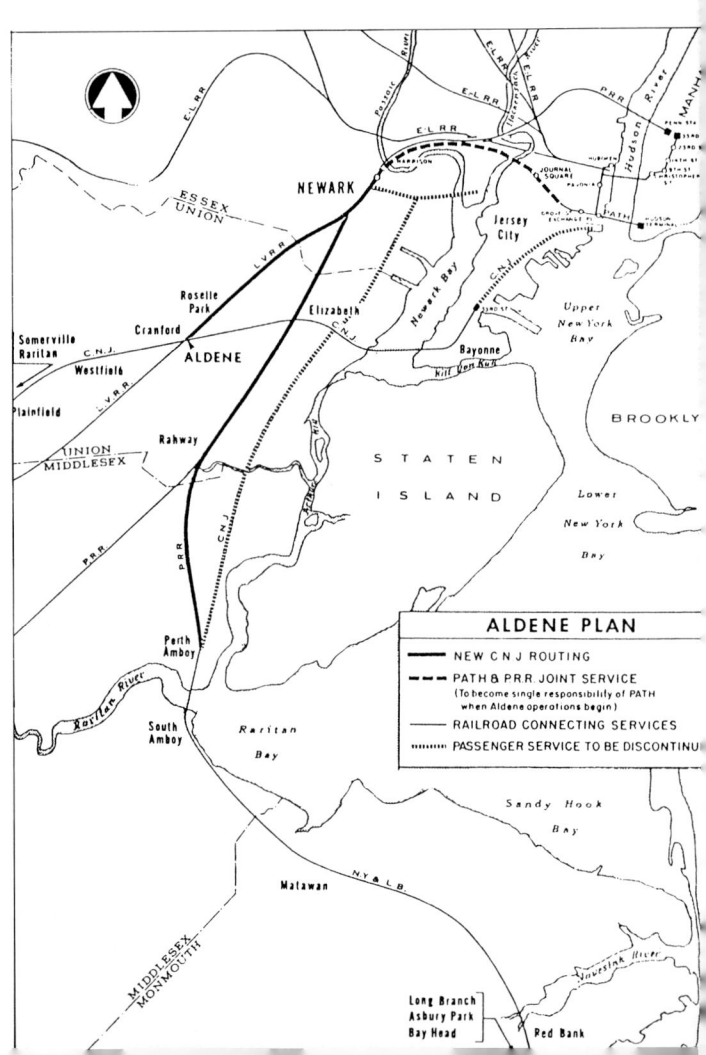

The ferry service provided by the Jersey Central RR from its terminal on the Jersey City waterfront to Liberty Street Manhattan was too great a burden for the RR to bear. The terminal location made it difficult to reach by any other means of transportation. Especially troublesome was the absence of Path service. Prohibitive costs prevented the development of any alternate to the Manhattan ferry service.

The bulk of commuters using the Jersey Central RR lived in communities from points west of Cranford. These commuters could also be served by routing the trains by means of a ramp at Aldene on the Lehigh Valley RR. This could bring the trains into Penn. Station Newark through an interchange at Hunter Tower. Lehigh Valley passenger trains had been doing this for decades. The shore service could also be brought into Newark by using the same tracks the Pennsylvania RR trains used to get to the shore. The only sizeable communities to be deprived of service between Cranford and Jersey City were Elizabeth and Bayonne. Elizabeth was already seved by the Penn. RR and Bayonne's objections were abated by agreeing to maintain a shuttle between Bayonne West 8th St. Station and Cranford with an intermediate stop at Elizabeth. However, after several years of marginal use by the citizens of Bayonne, the shuttle was discontinued.

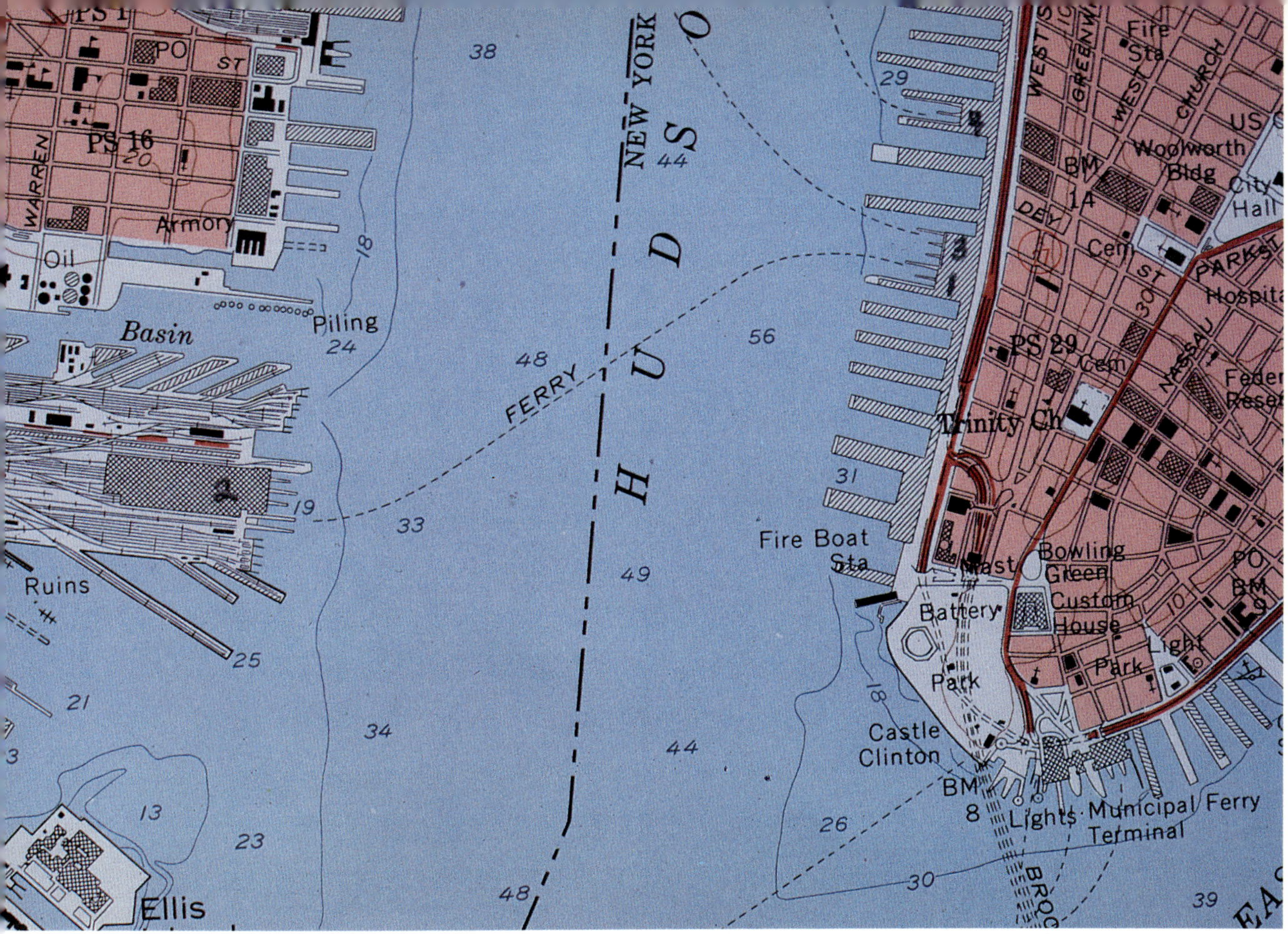

The Jersey Central ferry service ran from Liberty Street in Manhattan (1) to the RR terminal in Jersey City (2). Other RR ferry locations in Manhattan were the Erie Lackawanna at (4) and the New York Central West Shore at (3).

Ferry terminal entrance at Liberty Street Manhattan near the end of its long and productive career, 2/19/66. It was the Gateway to the Central RR of New Jersey, Reading Lines and at one time the Baltimore and Ohio RR.

Liberty Street ferry terminal lower level waiting room. At the far left off the photo a stairway led to the upper level gangways.

Ferry loaded to the limit at Liberty Street with anxious, evening rush hour commuters.

Ferry Cranford sailing towards Liberty Street. The ferry terminal is at the far left of the "twin towerless" lower Manhattan skyline. Chambers Street's well known radio row still existed.

Heading for the waiting trains, ferry "Elizabeth" makes a westbound crossing of the Hudson River.

The main concourse of the Jersey City terminal slumbers on a quiet Sunday morning. You are facing the ferry slip end of the building. The ticket office and waiting room are to the left. The baggage room is to the right.

Besides local commuter services, the station served as a gateway to more distant places in New Jersey, Pennsylvania and the South and West. For example the 5:57 PM "Queen of the Valley" served Western New Jersey and Pennsylvania by running as far as Allentown and in the early sixties carried cars that went through to Reading and Harrisburg. Note the open end of B&O business car 100 on the adjoining track. (W.J. Brennan)

The terminal also served the North Jersey Coast with trains to Bayhead Jct. - Pt. Pleasant. A service the Jersey Central shared with the Pennsylvania RR. The 5:02 PM train carried a first class parlor car, "Monmouth," with plush armchairs and beverage service. Admission was by monthly membership. (W.J. Brennan)

Besides the Jersey Central services, the Reading Lines maintained two first class commuter trains that served West Trenton, Jenkintown, Wayne Jct. and Broad Street Philadelphia. First out at 4:42 PM was the Crusader which at other times was equipped with a five car streamlined, double ended train.

These communities were also served by a second express the "Wall Street" which left exactly one hour later.

Under ventilated umbrella sheds varied power waits to speed the many trains westward to their destinations, as evidenced by the Reading FP-7's on the left, the Jersey Central Budd RDC's in the center and the Jersey Central's Fairbanks Morse Trainmaster 2402 on the right. Because of the selection of interesting motive power this terminal was a delightful place for the RR buff to do his train watching and photography.

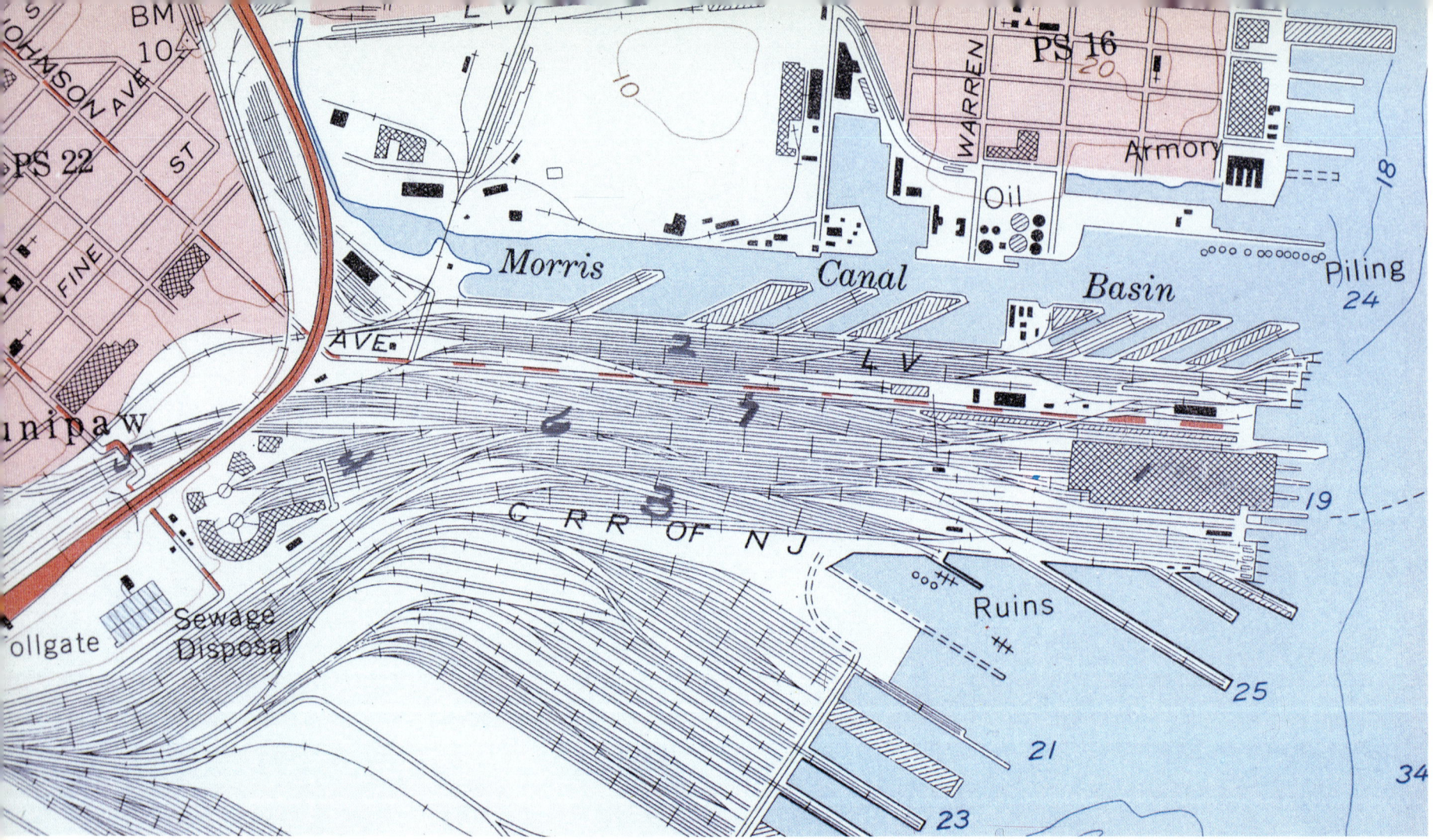

The locations in the terminal area are marked on the map as follows: (1) station platform; (2) L.V. car float yard; (3) Jersey Central car float yard; (4) Communipaw engine terminal; (5) Communipaw station and the jct. with the Newark Direct Line; (6) Main line; (7) Coach yard.

As the evening rush gets into full swing trainmaster 2407 leads out past sisters 2406 and 2413. Note the vehicles on the left occupying the space that tracks two and three should occupy. They were removed years ago so that the B&O bus connection from Manhattan could pull up alongside the limiteds bound for Washington D.C., Pittsburgh, Chicago and St. Louis. B&O RR service to New York ended in 1958.

As #321 the 4:43 PM train for Raritan heads out on a hot August 1966 evening. The new kids on the New York skyline, the twin towers of the World Trade Center, rise in uncompleted form over the myriad of signal bridges and semiphores that mark the approaches to the terminal.

F.M. #1500, the first of its type on the property, runs short end first as it snakes its way through the terminal interlocking. (W.J. Brennan)

The open end parlor car "Monmouth" passes terminal tower on its outbound run to the Jersey shore. Note the coach storage yard on the north side of the tracks and the piggyback unloading area on the south side.

Viewed from a signal bridge trainmaster #2404 leads an eastbound train into the south side of the terminal past tower "A" which governs the station interlocking.

RS-3 #1550 leads a two car local, which includes an arch roof combine. True to the ALCO tradition the engine acts as if it were an "honorary steam locomotive" as it departs under a heavy black plume of diesel oil exhaust.

On the flip side an eastbound train led by GP-7 #1521 heads onto terminal track #1 over rails that once served the plush limiteds of the B&O RR. The date however is April 12, 1966 so even this train is on borrowed time.

Acting like she is participating in the quarter mile drags, train 4101 the 4:11 PM Elizabethport local pretends she is a long distance express when all it's going to do is handle business on the Newark branch.

GP-7 1521, attired in its full striped regalia, leads train #1005 the 3:57 Elizabethport local past the coach yard.
(W.J. Brennan)

The same train departs on a sunnier day this time behind FP-7 #907 and friend.

A pair of FP-7's with the #902 on the point threads the terminal interlocking with the "Wall Street" bound for Philadelphia.

The Wall Street companion train on the Philly route "the Crusader" sallies forth from many storied Camelot under the exhaust of FP-7 #903.

The Crusader is most remembered for its consist which was built by Budd as a double ended five car train consisting of a single unit diner which served light meals, surrounded by two coaches and framed by two round end observation cars. This interior view is one of the observation ends.

The double ended observation permitted the train to shuttle back and forth between Jersey City and Philadelphia without turning the train. This feature intrigued the Canadian National Railroad which purchased the cars for service between Montreal and Quebec City. They were powered in Canada by FA's rather than FP-7's.

After running west from the terminal for almost a mile, the mainline curves southward at Communipaw station (1). It then runs in a straight line to Bayonne. The freight line enters the passenger main at (2). Van Nostrand Place is at (3). Claremont yard feeds the main at (4). Greenville station is located at (5) and East 45 St. Bayonne station is at location (6).

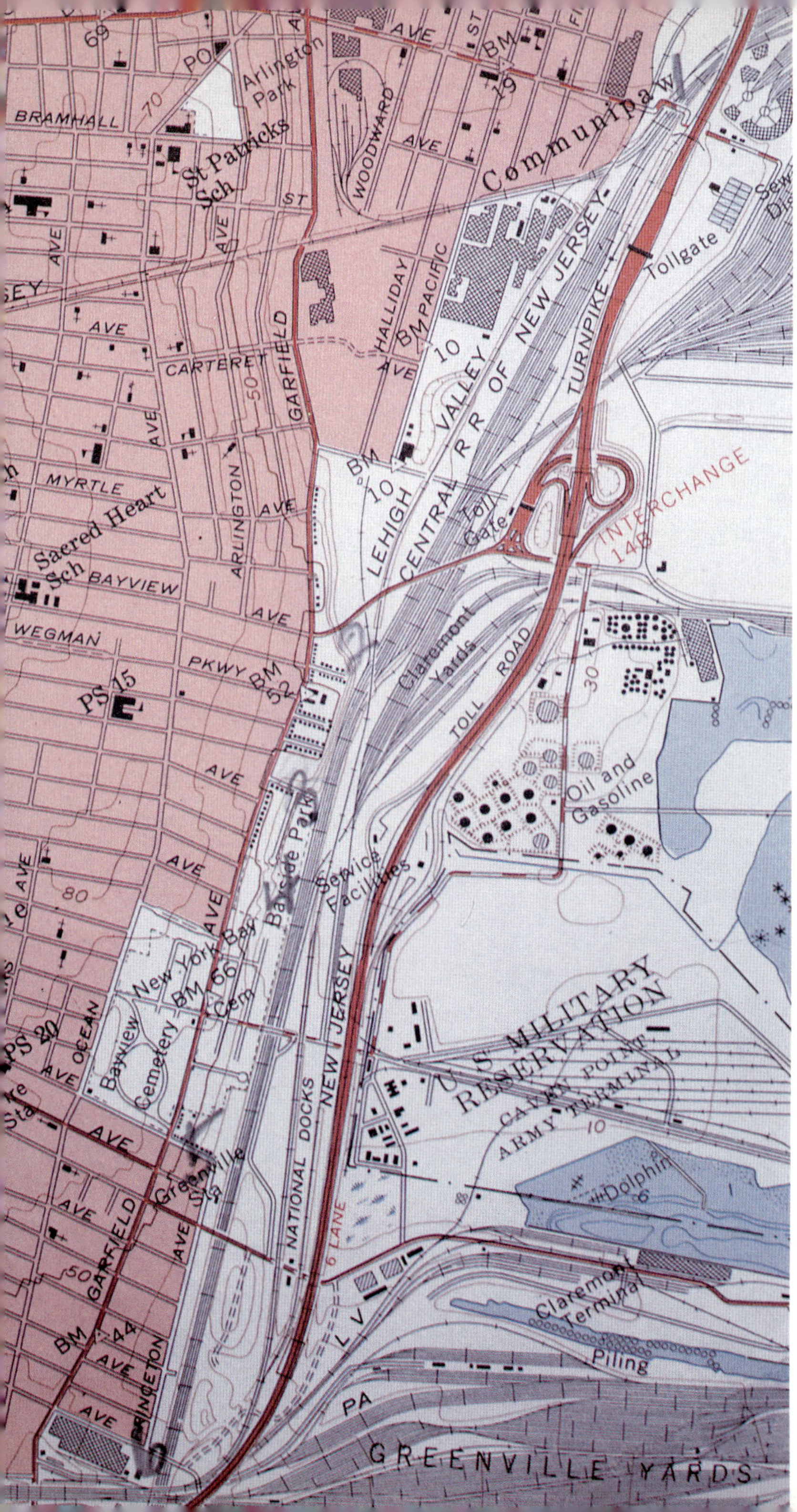

Baldwin RS-330 #1207 performs car washer service at Communipaw Jct. (W.J. Brennan)

The abandoned tower "C" at Communipaw once governed the Jct. of the direct line to Newark on the right with mainline from Bayonne on the left, stands as a silent sentinel for inbound morning trains powered by trainmaster 2412 and GP-7 1522.

"The Hunterdon Commuter" express regularly featured an air conditioned five car consist of RDC's. Departing at 5:17 PM, the first stop for this speedster is Bound Brook.

GP-7 #1524 rounds the Communipaw curve with the 5:49 PM North Jersey Coast express. The trestle in the background is the Weehawken branch connection with the New York Central.

Eastbound under the Weehawken trestle comes F.M. #1509 in a plain green wrapper.

At Van Nostrand Place station the freight trains enter the mainline, which this Reading powered freight is now doing. The freight yard is now as much history as the passenger service because Liberty State Park now occupies all of the former railroad property.

In this 1963 scene, 1509, fully dressed, slips through the Van Nostrand Place interlocking with a four car train.

SUBURBAN   MAINLINE   TRAINS

Jersey Central Lines

Passenger Service Completely Dieselized

EFFECTIVE OCT. 26, 1958

EASTERN STANDARD TIME

GP-7 #1522 passing Greenville station. The box on the nose of the unit contains train lighting equipment. With the steam generating boiler under the hood there was no room for the lighting equipment. The Boston and Maine and Chicago and Northwestern Geeps had a similar arrangement. (W.J. Brennan)

Nearing the Bayonne border, trainmaster #2411 leads a westbound, south of Greenville station.

Heading south as the crow flies, the line curves abruptly west at Bayonne West 8th street station. Location (1) marks the location of Greenville station and the point where the Penn line into Harsimus Cove crosses over. Three stations are located as follows: East 45th street is at location (2), 33rd street at (3), and 22nd street station at (4). The Bayonne West 8th street curve is at (5).

Trainmaster #2412 rushes a heavy consist past East 33rd Street Bayonne with train #3319, the 4:33 PM for Pt. Pleasant.

The 2:12 PM Raritan Clocker roars through the little used station at East 22nd Street Bayonne. Normally Budd RDC's, today's train is handled by a trainmaster using standard coaches.

Reading GP-35 #3630 waits in the hole at Bayonne yard as it is passed by a westbound passenger with 2413 leading the way. Today Hondas and Toyotas round the same curve.

2404 rounds the curve just east of Bayonne West 8th Street station. In the background is the yard office.

A ground level view of the same spot with a westbound headed by GP-7 #1530.

A westbound pauses at Bayonne West 8th Street station. Engine 1529, a GP-7, is on the head end.

The Saturday "Wall Street," train #1600, reduced to a set of Budd cars, speeds through Bayonne West 8th Street station. The infamous Bayonne drawbridge across Newark Bay looms in the background.

Geep 1521 climbs from a standing start the steep grade to the drawbridge.

Smoking FM #1509 passes "BV" tower Bayonne which governs the eastern approach to the drawbridge.

For Your Convenience

HOURLY
SERVICE
BY THE
CLOCK

between

Principal

Stations

and

NEW YORK

during

non-Commuter

hours

The westside of Newark drawbridge. The westbound track to the left of Budd RDC #556 was out of use for several years before the demise of passenger service. The right drawspan was the site of the infamous accident in 1958 when a passenger train went into the bay through the open span. Among the many fatalities was famous Yankee infielder "Snuffy" Sternweiss.

om Bayonne West 8th Street station (6) the line runs due west to Elizabethport. "BV" tower is at (7). Newark rawbridge is at (8). East Elizabethport tower is at (10).

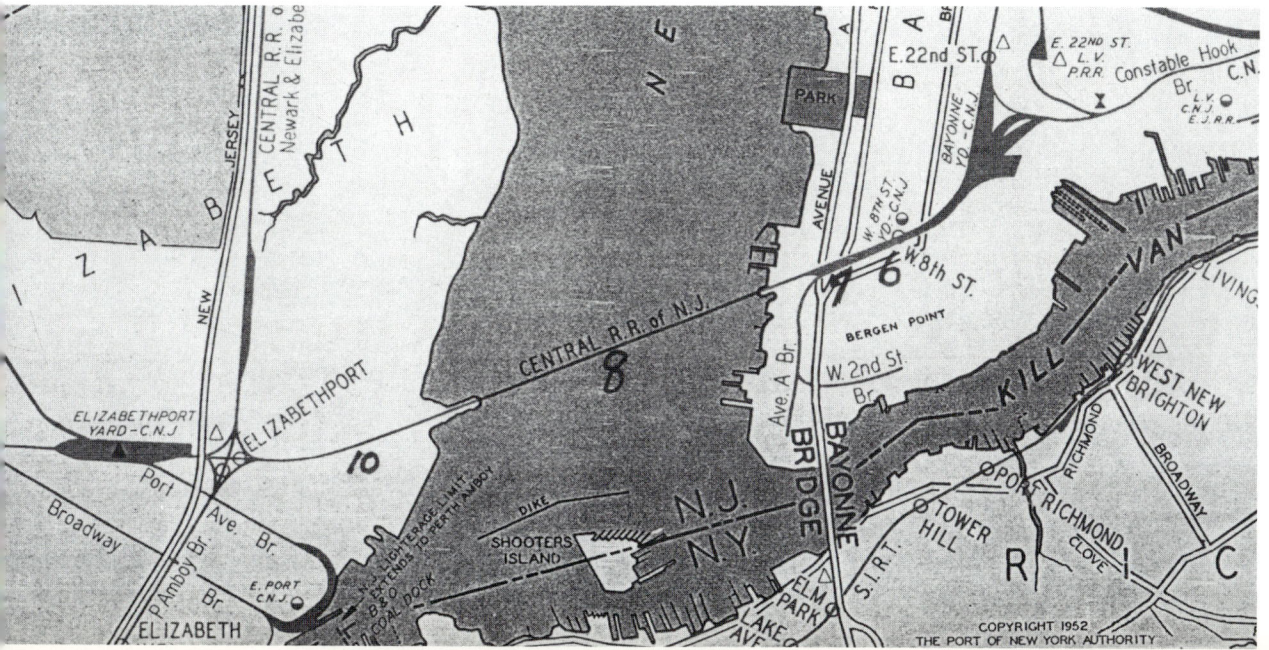

Plain GP-7 #1523 leads striped sister 1524 into Elizabethport pass the Jct. where the Pt. Pleasant trains diverge to the South, or the right of the photo.

Train #421 Bound for Raritan, with an Alco in the lead, slows through the final curve before Elizabethport station, arriving on time at 5:07 PM.

2413 Heads a Pt. Pleasant train through the same Jct. Newark Bay and the notorious drawbridge are in the background.

Miles from New York	EASTERN STANDARD TIME	RDC 3101	3305	3307	3319	3323	3117	3325	3327	3331	3333		
		AM	AM	Noon	PM	PM	PM	PM	PM	PM	PM		
.....	New York Liberty-Cortlandt St..Leave	6.00	8.28	12.00	4.20	4.50	‡4.50	5.09	5.45	6.45	9.35		
1.0	Jersey City Terminal........ Ar	6.11	8.45	12.12	4.33	5.02	‡5.02	5.23	5.57	6.57	9.53		
7.6	Bayonne, W. 8th St......... Lv	6.20	8.55	12.22	d4.43	a5.12	‡5a12	5.20	5.48	7.07	10.03		
.....	Newark { Broad St....... Lv	.....	‡8.40	‡12.10	‡4.30	‡5.05	5.05	‡5.10	‡5.50	‡6.50	‡9.48		
.....	{ Ferry St....... Lv	.....	‡8.42	‡12.12	‡4.32	‡5.07	5.07	‡5.12	‡5.52	‡6.52	‡9.50		
.....	{ East Ferry St... Lv	.....	‡8.44	‡12.14	‡4.34	‡5.09	5.09	‡5.14	‡5.54	‡6.54	‡9.52		
.....	Kearny................... Lv	.....	.....	.....	△3.56	‡4.59	4.59	.....	.....	.....	.....		
.....	Elizabeth................. Lv	‡6.01	‡8.47	‡11.55	‡4.34	‡5.12	5.12	‡5.31	‡5.57	‡6.55	‡9.55		
10.6	Elizabethport..............	6.26	9.03	12.30	4.50	□5.20	5.22	a5.38	6.12	7.13	10.09		
11.5	Elizabeth Ave.............. Ar												
12.4	Bayway....................	6.30											
17.9	Port Reading...............	6.36					5.32		6.20				
19.0	Sewaren...................						5.35		6.22				
20.2	Barber....................	6.39											
22.1	Perth Amboy...............	6.44	9.19	12.46	5.05		5.42		6.27	7.28	10.24		
24.1	South Amboy...............	6.48	9.23	12.50	5.09		5.46		6.31	7.32	10.28		
28.1	Cliffwood..................						5.52						
29.3	Matawan...................	6.56	9.32	12.56	5.18	5.45	5.55	6.03	6.40	7.40	10.37		
31.1	Hazlet....................					5.49			6.44	7.44	10.40		
35.3	Middletown................				5.25	5.55		6.11	6.49	7.48	10.43		
39.1	Red Bank..................		9.45	1.03	5.33	6.02		6.18	6.54	7.54	10.49		
41.5	Little Silver—Oceanport....				5.38	6.07		6.24	7.00	7.58	10.54		
43.0	Monmouth Park............												
45.1	Long Branch................		9.56	1.20	5.45	6.14		6.30	7.06	8.04	11.00		
47.3	Elberon—Oakhurst.........		9.59	1.24	5.49	6.18		6.34	7.09	8.08	11.04		
49.3	Allenhurst (Interlaken)......		10.03	1.28	5.53	6.22		6.38	7.13	8.12	11.08		
50.1	N. Asbury Park-Wanamassa..			1.31				6.40		8.15	11.11		
50.8	Asbury Park-Ocean Grove...		10.11	1.34	5.57	6.26		6.43	7.17	8.18	11.14		
51.7	Bradley Beach (Neptune).....		10.14	1.37				6.46	7.20	8.21	11.17		
52.6	Avon (Neptune City)........		10.16	1.40				6.49	7.23				
53.4	Belmar...................		10.20	1.43	6.02	6.32		6.52	7.25	8.25	11.21		Through train from Newark
55.5	Spring Lake-Spring Lake Hgts.		10.24	1.47	6.07	6.36		6.55	7.29	8.29	11.25		
56.9	Sea Girt..................			1.50	6.09	6.39		6.59	7.32				
57.6	Manasquan................		10.28	1.53	6.12	6.42		7.03	7.35	8.33	11.29		
59.6	Point Pleasant Beach........		10.34	1.59	6.17	6.47		7.08	7.39	8.37	11.33		
60.7	Bay Head Junction..........		10.40	2.04	6.22	6.52		7.14	7.44	8.42	11.37		
	Arrive	AM	AM	PM	PM	PM		PM	PM	PM	PM		

MONDAYS THRU FRIDAYS except Nov. 8, 24, Dec. 26, Jan. 2, Feb. 22

This map shows the Elizabethport station area. The main line runs right to left on the map. The Newark branch runs north from the station. The branch to the Amboys runs south from the station. The Jersey Central shops are to the northeast of the station, the freight yard parallels the mainline at the left.

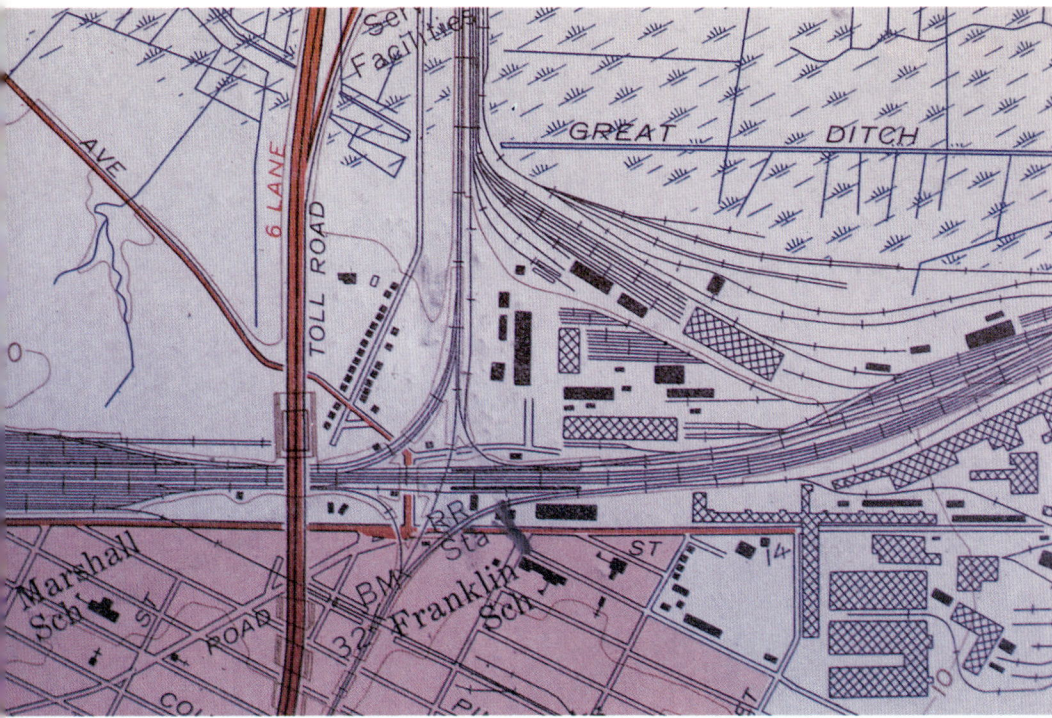

The "Hunterdon Commuter" express accelerates through Elizabethport on its dash to Hampton.

Trainmasters 2408 and 2409 from Pt. Pleasant and Raritan respectively head for the drawbridge while a westbound freight passes on the right. (W.J. Brennan)

F.M. #1510 slows for Elizabethport station with Train #419 the 4:12 PM Raritan Clocker. Elizabethport shops are in the background.

FARES BETWEEN NEW YORK AND STATIONS IN SUBURBAN TERRITORY

The Federal Tax of 10% is not included in fares shown below. No tax applies on Commutation Tickets or on One-Way Tickets where the fare is 60 cents or less.

Subject to Change	One Way	Standard Monthly Commutation	Unlimited Monthly Commutation	Weekly Commutation
Communipaw	$0.45	$16.50	$19.80	$4.65
Van Nostrand Place	.45	16.50	19.80	4.65
Greenville	.45	16.50	19.80	4.65
East 45th Street	.49	16.50	19.80	4.65
East 33rd Street	.53	17.70	21.10	5.00
East 22nd Street	.54	18.85	22.40	5.30
West 8th Street	.58	20.05	23.70	5.65
Elizabethport	.65	23.20	27.20	6.50
Spring Street	.68	24.15	28.30	6.80
Elizabeth	.72	25.15	29.40	7.05
Elmora Avenue	.74	26.15	30.50	7.35
Lorraine	.78	26.15	30.50	7.35
Roselle-Roselle Pk.	.78	27.15	31.60	7.60
Cranford	.86	28.60	33.20	8.00
Garwood	.96	29.10	33.75	8.15
Westfield	.96	30.05	34.85	8.45
Fanwood-Scotch Pls.	1.05	31.05	35.95	8.70
Netherwood-Plfd.	1.05	31.40	36.35	8.80
Plainfield-No. Plfd.	1.12	31.80	36.80	8.90
Grant Ave., Plfd.	1.12	32.20	37.20	9.00
Clinton Ave., Plfd.	1.23	32.55	37.60	9.10
Dunellen	1.23	32.95	38.05	9.25
Middlesex	1.32	33.70	38.90	9.45
Bound Brook	1.43	34.45	39.70	9.65
Manville-Finderne	1.50	35.30	40.65	9.90
Somerville	1.62	35.85	41.30	10.05
Raritan	1.62	36.15	41.60	10.10
North Branch	1.82	37.00	42.55	10.35
White House	2.01	38.40	44.10	10.75
Lebanon	2.10	38.95	44.70	10.90
Annandale	2.21	39.15	44.90	10.95
High Bridge	2.29	39.35	45.15	11.00
Glen Gardner	2.41	39.60	45.45	11.10
Hampton	2.50	39.80	45.65	11.15

For COMMUTATION TICKET PRIVILEGES see Page 31.

Later in the evening the "Westfielder" bound for Scotch Plains on the same track races past the E-Port station baggage elevators.

GP-7 #1521 with train #421 pauses at E-port before crossing the diamond in the foreground where the Newark-Elizabethport shuttle crosses the mainline.

On a crisp winter day the Saturday only 3:17 PM shuttle arrives at E-Port, crossing the mainline on its trip from Newark.

From Elizabethport Jct. at the lower left. The southern portion of the Newark branch runs north in a straight line through swampland paralleling the New Jersey Turnpike and Newark Airport. The Airport runway is on the top center portion of the map.

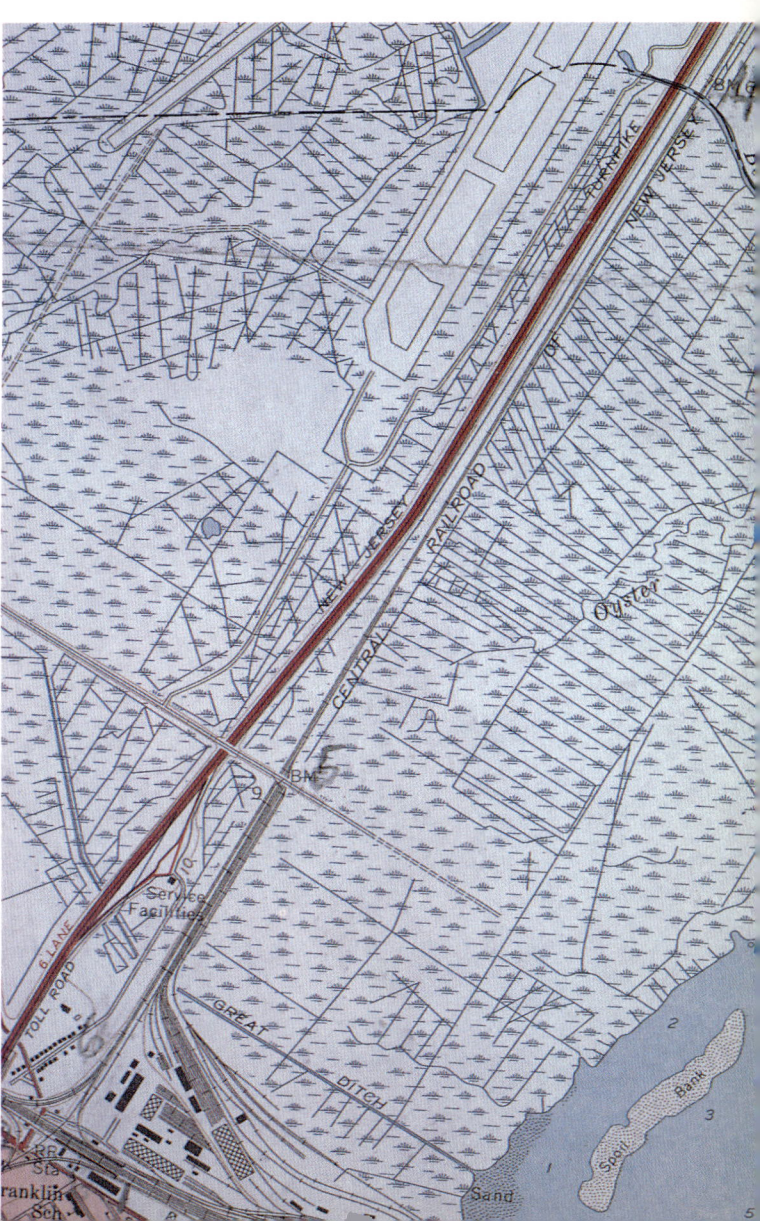

Newark shuttle waiting at its E-Port pocket platform. The station is triangular with the mainline platforms in the background and the shore platforms to the right.

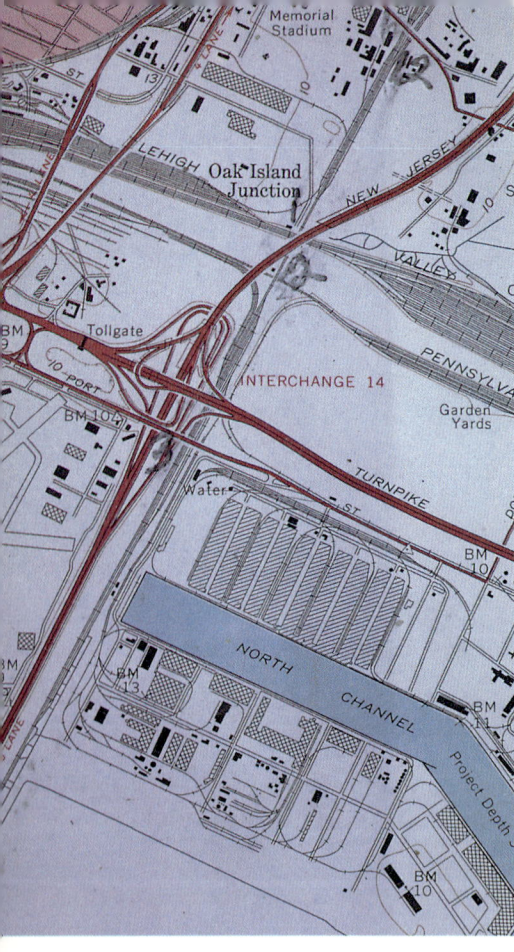

At the northern end of the airport the line curves slightly to the east and crosses the Penn. RR's Harsimus cove line at grade. Harsimus Cove yard is now a shopping center.

When the moment was right Newark shuttles would dare to challenge Newark Airport's planes and parallel New Jersey Turnpike's cars to a test of speed. No mean feat on the bouncy, wavy, though straight trackwork that traverses this swamp. From my own experience I can testify that they more than held their own.

North of the airport at Oak Island Jct. the Jersey Central bisects at grade the Pennsylvania Railroad freight line into Carney Meadows Yard. The tower governing the Jct. was manned by "P Company" employees. Casting a pall on the railroad scene is the competition in the form of the Jersey Turnpike.

The line to Kearny and the line to Newark split at location (6). Kearny is in the direction marked (7). Brills Jct. is at (5). East Ferry Street station is at (4). Ferry Street station is at (3). The branch crosses Pennsylvania station Newark at (2) and the Jersey Central station in Newark is located at (1).

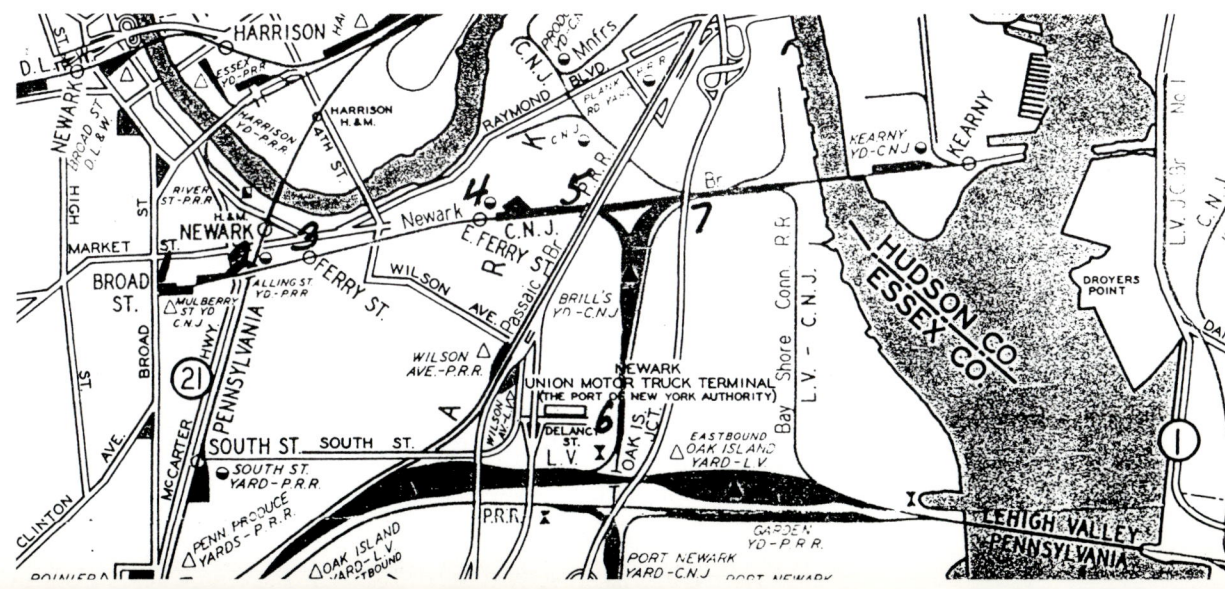

The west leg of the wye called Brills Jct. connected the branch to Elizabethport with the truncated Newark-Jersey City direct line. A Budd RDC set led by #557 passes Brills Jct. tower on its way to Newark.

Elizabethport bound shuttle leaves East Ferry Street station in this October 1966 scene. (W.J. Brennan)

Train #7247 the 9:43 AM shuttle to Elizabethport departs Newark station from track #2.

Before arriving at the Jersey Central Station in Newark the branch crosses the Pennsylvania RR at the west end of the platforms of the Pennsy's Broad Street Newark station.

NEW YORK AND FLEMINGTON
MONDAYS THRU FRIDAYS
EXCEPT NOV. 4, 27, DEC. 25, JAN. 1, FEB. 23

Read Down			Read Up
203 MC 31	Miles	EASTERN STANDARD TIME	202 MC 32
PM		Lv New York Ar	AM
5.03	0.0	....Liberty—Cortlandt St.....	8.22
5.17	1.0	....Jersey City........	8.06
‡5.20	7.6	....Bayonne, W. 8th St....	‡8.32
‡5.11		....Newark (Broad St.)....	‡8.44
n5.34	12.5	....Elizabeth........	8.15
5.39	24.0	..Plainfield—No. Plainfield....	7.58
5.52	31.2	....Bound Brook.......	7.31
5.58	35.6	Ar} Somerville (CNJ Station) .{Lv	7.25
6.02	35.6	Lv} {Ar	7.25
	36.8	Ar} Raritan (CNJ Station)...{Lv	7.22
	36.8	Lv} {Ar	7.17
M6.17	44.1	....Flagtown (Post Office).....	R7.02
M6.31	48.6	....Neshanic (Post Office)....	R6.48
M6.45	54.4	.......{Three Bridges}.....	R6.34
		{R. R. Smith's Store}	
M6.52	58.0	...Flemington (CNJ Station)...	R6.27
PM		Ar Lv	AM

NO SERVICE ON SATURDAYS, SUNDAYS OR
Nov. 4, 27, Dec. 25, Jan. 1, Feb. 23.

NEWARK AND KEARNY
MONDAYS THRU FRIDAYS
EXCEPT NOV. 27, DEC. 25, JAN. 1, FEB. 23

Read Down						Read Up	
7908	7906	Will run only Nov. 4	7904	7902	EASTERN STANDARD TIME	Miles	7909	7913
AM	AM		AM	AM	Lv Ar		PM	PM
8.05	7.40		7.05	6.25	Newark {Broad St......	3.3	4.05	5.37
8.07	7.42		7.07	6.27	Newark {Ferry St.......	2.7	4.03	5.35
8.09	7.44		7.08	6.29	Newark {E. Ferry St.....	2.0	4.01	5.33
	7.47				Newark Transfer.......	0.8	3.58	
8.13	7.50		7.13	6.33	Kearny...........	0.0	3.56	5.28
AM	AM		AM	AM	Ar Lv		PM	PM

NO SERVICE ON SATURDAYS, SUNDAYS OR
Nov. 27, Dec. 25, Jan. 1, Feb. 23.

EXPLANATION OF REFERENCE MARKS
a—Stops on notice to take passengers.
M—Arriving time of connecting Motor-coach, change at Somerville.
R—Leaving time of connecting Motor-coach, change at Raritan.
‡—Leaving or arriving time of connecting train, change at Elizabeth.
n—Leaving or arriving time of connecting train; change at Elizabethport and Elizabeth.
A. M. time in light-face type.   P. M. time in bold face type.

Track #2 is the only track used by the shuttles. Track #3 was used only during rush hour. Tracks #1 & #4 were removed after the direct line was severed.

Newark station facade on the Broad Street side. An imposing edifice for such a minor operation.

Standard consist used during the rush hour backs into Newark past Brills Jct. tower. This train operated as #1007 a 4:12 PM local from Jersey City to E-Port.

The backup move for train #9501 passing the tower located on the east leg of the Brills Jct. wye.

The same move backing up to the bridge leading into Kearny. Note the missing track and the remains of Newark Transfer station left over from when the Direct Line to Jersey City was in service.

Train #9501 led by GP-7 #1521 waits to load passengers at Kearny. Western Electric provided most of the riders. It departed Kearny at 4:59 PM bound for Plainfield. (W.J. Brennan)

As a deadhead backing up the Newark Branch to Kearny crosses Oak Island Jct. a Lehigh Valley freight passes overhead.

Empty backup move for train #9501 passing the Newark Airport station. Needless to say, this is not the way most people got to the airport.

Train #9500 backing into E-Port for its run to Kearny. This train originated in Plainfield. On arriving from Plainfield the train uses the northwest leg of the Jct. and then backs south into the shuttle pocket to load passengers.

The south side of Elizabethport station. On the left is train #7217 the 5:18 PM arrival from Newark, powered by GP-7 #1529. On the right is train #3323 the 5:02 PM out of Jersey City with a 6:49 arrival in Bay Head Jct. This day trainmaster #2413 did the honors.

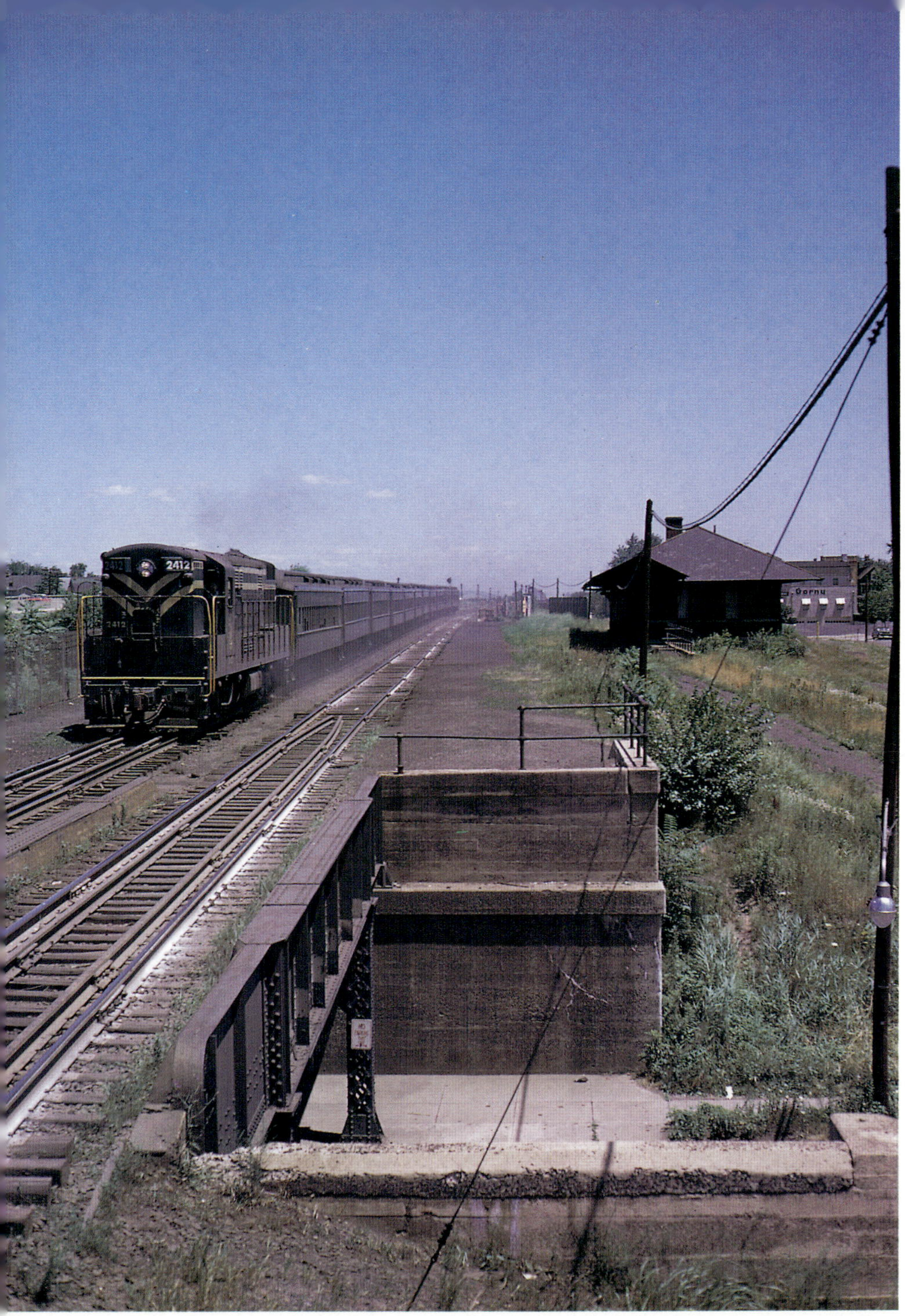

Train #3355 passes Elizabeth Avenue station, at full cry as the British would say, bound for Bay Head Jct. with trainmaster 2412 on the point.

GP-7 #1522 glides through Elizabeth Avenue station with train #3361, the Saturday only, 4:14 PM out of Jersey City. The station building was closed and the platforms were in use as a rush hour conditional stop.

Train #3344 passing a local freight between Bayway and Elizabeth Avenue headed by unstriped trainmaster #2409. The Jersey Turnpike is on the left.

1-DAY Round Trip, ONE WAY and COMMUTATION FARES										
	Between NEW YORK and					Between NEWARK and				
Subject to Change	1-Day Round Trip, see Note	One-Way	Standard Monthly Commutation	Unlimited Monthly Commutation	Weekly Commutation	1-Day Round Trip, see Note	One-Way	Standard Monthly Commutation	Unlimited Monthly Commutation	Weekly Commutation
South Amboy	$1.95	$1.30	$35.25	$40.60	$9.85	$1.50	$0.98	$24.85	$27.60	$6.90
Cliffwood	2.30	1.53	36.75	42.30	10.30	1.80	1.18	26.50	29.40	7.35
Matawan	2.30	1.53	37.45	43.05	10.50	1.80	1.18	27.25	30.25	7.60
Hazlet	2.50	1.65	37.70	43.35	10.55	2.00	1.31	27.60	30.65	7.70
Middletown	2.65	1.74	39.10	44.90	10.95	2.35	1.55	29.30	32.55	8.15
Red Bank	3.00	1.98	39.95	45.85	11.20	2.50	1.64	30.15	33.50	8.40
Little Silver—Oceanport	3.15	2.10	40.80	46.80	11.40	2.70	1.78	31.05	34.45	8.65
Long Branch	3.50	2.32	41.35	47.40	11.55	3.05	2.02	31.90	35.40	8.85
Elberon—Oakhurst	3.50	2.32	41.75	47.85	11.70	3.20	2.12	32.70	36.30	9.10
Allenhurst (Interlaken)	3.65	2.43	41.95	48.05	11.75	3.40	2.26	32.95	36.60	9.15
N. Asbury Park—Wanamassa	3.85	2.55	41.95	48.05	11.75	3.40	2.26	32.95	36.60	9.15
Asbury Park—Ocean Grove	3.85	2.55	42.05	48.15	11.75	3.40	2.26	33.10	36.75	9.20
Bradley Beach (Neptune)	3.85	2.55	42.15	48.25	11.80	3.60	2.37	33.25	36.90	9.25
Avon (Neptune City)	4.00	2.64	42.20	48.35	11.80	3.60	2.37	33.35	37.05	9.30
Belmar	4.00	2.64	42.30	48.45	11.85	3.60	2.37	33.45	37.15	9.30
Spring Lake—Spring Lake Hgt's	4.20	2.78	42.50	48.65	11.90	3.75	2.50	33.65	37.35	9.35
Sea Girt	4.20	2.78	42.60	48.75	11.90	3.90	2.60	33.75	37.45	9.40
Manasquan	4.35	2.89	42.65	48.85	11.95	3.90	2.60	33.80	37.55	9.40
Point Pleasant Beach	4.35	2.89	42.85	49.05	12.00	4.15	2.74	34.00	37.75	9.45
Bay Head Junction	4.55	3.01	42.90	49.10	12.00	4.15	2.74	34.10	37.85	9.50

NOTE.—ONE DAY ROUND TRIP TICKETS MAY BE USED AS FOLLOWS:
MONDAYS THRU FRIDAYS (Except Holidays):
Tickets sold TO New York and Newark.
Going on date of sale, tickets are good on trains:
Arriving New York After 9.15 A.M.
Arriving Newark After 9.08 A.M.
Returning on date of sale, tickets are good on trains:
	BEFORE	AFTER
Leaving New York	4.25 P.M.	6.21 P.M.
Leaving Jersey City	4.35 P.M.	6.30 P.M.
Leaving Newark	4.31 P.M.	6.30 P.M.

Tickets sold FROM New York and Newark.
Going on date of sale, tickets are good on trains leaving New York and Newark BEFORE 4.30 A.M. and AFTER 8.25 A.M.
Returning on date of sale, tickets are good on all trains.
SATURDAYS, SUNDAYS & HOLIDAYS: Tickets are good on all trains on date of sale.
One-Way tickets (Year limit, unlimited in New Jersey) are sold daily, and are good in coaches only.
Standard Monthly tickets are good for an unlimited number of rides on weekdays, Mondays thru Fridays, during calendar month for which issued (except days celebrated as Holidays, namely: New Year's Day, Memorial Day, Independence Day, Labor Day, Thanksgiving Day and Christmas Day).
Unlimited Monthly tickets are good for an unlimited number of rides during calendar month for which issued.
Weekly—12-Trip Weekly tickets to and from stations on The New York and Long Branch Railroad, good for twelve single continuous rides in either direction, valid Sunday thru Saturday, during calendar week for which issued.
Weekly tickets to and from stations on The Central Railroad Company of New Jersey, good for an unlimited number of rides in either direction, valid Sunday thru Saturday, during calendar week for which issued.

Bound for the shore #1516 passes "WY" tower and Bascule Bridge in July 1963.

#2413 is having no trouble with light, Saturday afternoon train #3359 as it passes one of the refineries for which Bayway is noted. This is why this is still a very active branch even though the passenger trains are long gone.

Train #3355 passing one of the small halts, Sewaren. It's used only during the rush hour.

BETWEEN ELIZABETHPORT AND NEWARK
Eastern Standard Time

Train No.	Leave Elizabethport	Arrive East Ferry Street	Arrive Ferry Street	Arrive Broad Street	Train No.	Leave Broad Street	Leave Ferry Street	Arrive East Ferry Street	Arrive Elizabethport
MONDAYS THRU FRIDAYS Except Nov. 8, 24, Dec. 26, Jan. 2, Feb. 22					**MONDAYS THRU FRIDAYS** Except Nov. 8, 24, Dec. 26, Jan. 2, Feb. 22				
					7902	6.25	6.27	6.29	6.49
A7200	6.08	6.17	6.19	6.21	7201	7.11	7.13	7.15	7.24
C7202	6.54	7.03	7.05	7.07	7203	8.40	8.42	8.44	8.53
D7204	7.04	7.16	7.18	7.20	7205	9.40	9.42	9.44	9.53
7206	7.28	7.37	7.39	7.41	7207	12.10	12.12	12.14	12.23
F7208	7.45	7.56	7.59	8.02	7209	1.10	1.12	1.14	1.23
G7210	8.31	8.40	8.42	8.44	7211	3.10	3.12	3.14	3.23
7212	8.57	9.06	9.08	9.10	7213	4.11	4.13	4.15	4.24
7214	10.01	10.10	10.12	10.14	7215	4.30	4.32	4.34	4.43
7216	12.30	12.39	12.41	12.43	H7229	4.49	4.51	4.53	5.03
7218	2.01	2.10	2.12	2.14	7217	5.05	5.07	5.09	5.18
7220	3.26	3.35	3.37	3.39	7219	5.11	5.13	5.15	5.24
7100	4.39	5.01	5.03	5.05	7221	5.45	5.47	5.49	5.58
7222	6.03	6.12	6.14	6.16	7221	6.40	6.42	6.44	6.53
7224	7.02	7.11	7.13	7.15	7223	9.48	9.50	9.52	10.01
7226	10.14	10.25	10.27	10.29	7401	10.55	10.57	10.59	11.10
SATURDAYS & ELECTION DAY Nov. 8 ONLY					**SATURDAYS & ELECTION DAY Nov. 8 ONLY**				
					7241	6.25	6.27	6.29	6.38
7240	5.55	6.04	6.06	6.08	7243	7.15	7.17	7.19	7.28
7242	6.54	7.04	7.06	7.08	7245	8.40	8.42	8.44	8.53
E7244	7.55	8.06	8.08	8.10	7247	9.43	9.45	9.47	9.56
7246	9.01	9.10	9.12	9.14	7249	12.10	12.12	12.14	12.23
7248	10.02	10.11	10.13	10.15	7251	1.10	1.12	1.14	1.23
7250	12.30	12.39	12.41	12.43	7253	2.10	2.12	2.14	2.23
7252	2.35	2.44	2.46	2.48	7255	3.00	3.02	3.04	3.13
7254	3.17	3.27	3.29	3.31	7257	4.10	4.12	4.14	4.24
7256	4.51	5.00	5.02	5.04	7259	5.10	5.12	5.14	5.23
7258	5.30	5.39	5.41	5.43	7261	6.12	6.14	6.16	6.25
7260	8.02	8.11	8.13	8.15	7263	6.50	6.52	6.54	7.03
7262	10.25	10.35	10.37	10.39	7265	9.43	9.45	9.47	9.56
					7267	10.55	10.57	10.59	11.08
SUNDAYS & Nov. 24, Dec. 26, Jan. 2, Feb. 22 ONLY					**SUNDAYS & Nov. 24, Dec. 26, Jan. 2, Feb. 22 ONLY**				
7270	7.13	7.23	7.25	7.27	7271	8.50	8.52	8.54	9.03
7272	10.02	10.11	10.13	10.15	7273	10.40	10.42	10.44	10.53
7274	11.02	11.11	11.13	11.15	7275	12.10	12.12	12.14	12.23
7276	1.02	1.11	1.13	1.15	7277	1.40	1.42	1.44	1.53
7278	2.02	2.11	2.13	2.15	7279	3.10	3.12	3.14	3.23
7280	5.24	5.33	5.35	5.37	7281	4.10	4.12	4.14	4.23
7282	8.22	8.31	8.33	8.35	7283	5.05	5.07	5.09	5.18
7284	9.27	9.37	9.39	9.41	7285	7.10	7.12	7.14	7.23
					7287	10.10	10.12	10.14	10.23

A—Stops at Newark Airport 6.12 A.M.
C—Stops at Newark Airport 6.58 A.M.
D—Stops at Newark Airport 7.10 A.M.
E—Stops at Newark Airport 7.59 A.M.
F—Stops at Newark Airport 7.50 A.M.
G—Stops at Newark Airport 8.35 A.M.
H—Stops at Newark Airport 4.58 P.M.
A.M.—Light face type.   P.M.—Bold face type.
f—Stops on notice to take or leave passengers.

Train #3354 due for a 9:13 PM arrival in Jersey City heads north bound at Port Reading. GP-7 #1523 is about to cross the diamond with the Reading RR on this Saturday morning in March of 1967.

Barber, which has one of the more interesting stations, sees the 2:12 PM out of Jersey City rush past.

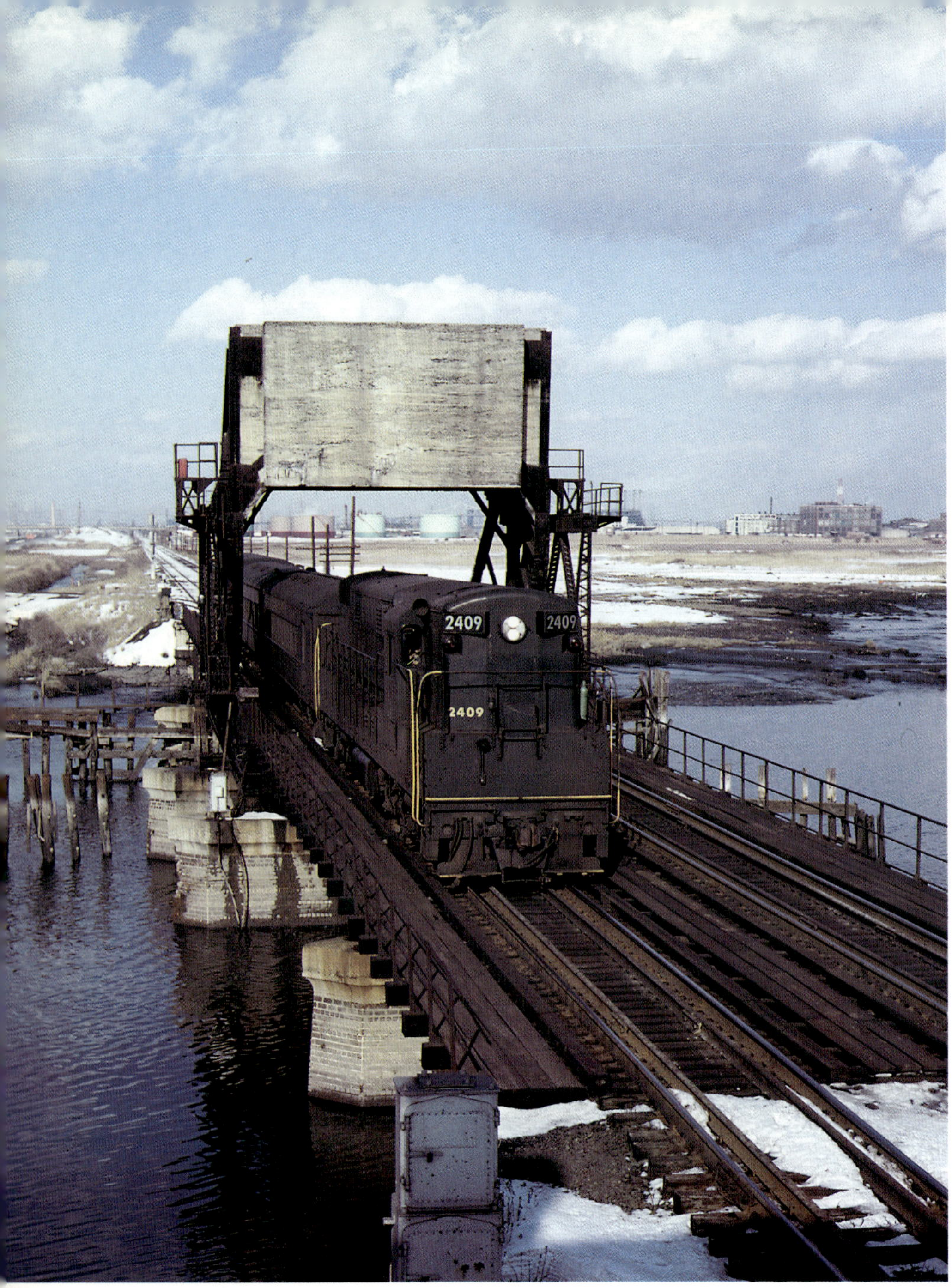

SEASHORE
TRAINS

EFFECTIVE

OCTOBER 30, 1966

(Corrected November 3, 1966)

EASTERN STANDARD TIME

#2409, busy this winter day in 1967, brings #3359 the Saturday afternoon shore train into Barber, over one of the several drawbridges on this branch.

Perth Amboy where the Pennsylvania RR trains merge with the Jersey Central trains to provide joint service for the North Jersey coast. After the Aldene plan went into effect trains from both RR's run jointly from Newark and come through this junction from the left. Only freight service is still provided on this branch from Elizabethport. Train #3359 with the ever present 2413 demonstrates what it used to be.

BETWEEN **NEW YORK** AND
PHILADELPHIA, EASTON, BETHLEHEM
ALLENTOWN, READING, HARRISBURG

EFFECTIVE OCTOBER 25, 1959

EASTERN STANDARD TIME

"BU" tower which governs Elizabethport Junction is located south of the mainline just west of the point where the Newark branch crosses the main. 1509 crosses over to platform at the station. All eastbound locals use this crossover.

Back on the mainline the following locations are marked on the map as follows: Elizabethport station on the far right is at (1). The line then crosses the Newark branch at (2) and passes "BU" tower at (3). (4) marks the west end of the yard and "GW" tower. Spring Street station is at (5 & 6). The line then curves slightly to the southwest at (7). It passes under the Pennsylvania RR's New York Division at (8) and Elizabeth station at (9). The Cherry Street overpass is at (10) and the original milepost is at (11). Elmora Avenue station is at (12).

#1511 with the "Queen City Bee" buzzes by Elizabethport a few days before the curtain rings down on Jersey City operations.

"GW" tower which is located between Elizabeth and Elizabethport serves the west end of E-Port yard. RS-3 #1549 leads a surprise consist today, because this Saturday only 3:12 PM Raritan Clocker is normally scheduled to have RDC's.

A view of Elizabeth station from the Pennsylvania RR southbound platform taken in April 1967 just before the Aldene plan went into effect. These days the automobiles in the foreground would make a respectable car show.

Train #1005 which had terminated at Elizabethport and has pulled up past the turnpike west of "BU" tower. It will now back up the Newark branch to Kearny using the west leg of the wye.

MONDAYS to FRIDAYS incl. except Nov. 4, 27, Dec. 25, Jan. 1, Feb. 23

Eastern Standard Time WESTBOUND	401	601	3101	403	441	RDC 405	3305	RDC 407	409	RDC 411	RDC 413	3307	107	RDC 415	1205	417	801	RDC 4101	419	1005	3319	421
	AM	AM	AM	AM	AM	AM	AM	AM	AM	AM	Noon	Noon	PM	PM	PM	PM	PM	PM	PM	PM	PM	PM
New York....Leave Liberty-Cort'dt St.	6.17	6.35	6.35	7.03	7.30	8.00	8.33	9.00	10.00	11.00	12.00	12.00	1.00	2.00	2.30	3.00	3.45	4.00	4.00	4.00	4.20	4.30
Jersey City Term..	6.29	6.47	6.46	7.18	7.43	8.12	8.45	9.12	10.12	11.12	12.12	12.14	1.12	2.12	2.42	3.12	3.57	4.11	4.12	4.22	4.33	4.45
Communipaw....				7.21	7.46										2.45		4.00			4.25		
Van Nostrand Pl..					7.48																	
Greenville.......	6.35		6.52	7.25	7.50										2.49		4.03			4.28		
East 45th St....	6.38		6.55	7.28						"RARITAN CLOCKER"	"RARITAN CLOCKER"									4.31		
East 33rd St.. (Bay-	6.40		6.57	7.31	7.55	8.16		9.19				12.19			2.52		4.07			4.33		
East 22nd St..{onne			6.59	7.34	7.57	8.20											4.09			4.36		4:55
West 8th St...)	6.44	6.56	7.02	7.37	8.04	8.23	8.55	9.22	10.22	11.22	12.22	12.24	1.22	2.22	2.57	3.22	4.12	4.20	4.22	4.39		4.59
Newark (Broad St.) Lv	6:25	6:25		7:11				8:40	9:40			12:10	1:10			3:10			4:12			4:49
Kearny..........Lv																					3c56	
Elizabethport...	6.50		7.0S	①7.52	8.10	8.29	9.01	9.28	10.28	11.28	12.28	12.30	1.28	2.28	3.03	3.28	4.18	4.27	4.28	4.44	4.50	5.07
Spring Street......	6.53																					
Elizabeth.........	6.56	7.04		7.56	8.18	8.33		9.32	10.32	11.32	12.32	(thru to Allentown)	1.32	2.32		3.32	4.22		4.32			5.11
Elmora Avenue......	6.59			7.59	8.22	8.35														4.35		5.14
Lorraine.........	7.01																4.25					
Roselle-Roselle Pk..	7.04			8.03		8.37		9.36	10.36	11.36	12.36		1.36	2.36		3.36	4.27	4.30	4.38			5.18
Cranford.........	7.09			8.07		8.41		9.40	10.40	11.40	12.40		1.40	2.40		3.40	4.34	4.34	4.42			5.23
Garwood..........				8.10		8.43										3.42			4.45			
Westfield........	7.14	7.11		8.13		8.45		9.44	10.44	11.44	12.44		1.44	2.44		3.45			4.48			5.28
Fanwood-Scotch Pls..				8.17										2.48		3.50			4.53			5.33
Netherwood-Plfd...				8.19												3.53			4.56			5.36
Plainfld.-No. Plfd..	7.21	7.18		8.22		8.52		9.51	10.51	11.51	12.51		1.51	2.52		3.57			4.59			5.39
Grant Ave., Plfd...	7.23			8.24												4.00			5.02			
Clinton Ave., Plfd..	7.26			8.26																		
Dunellen.........	7.29	7.23		8.29		8.57		9.56	10.56	11.56	12.56		1.56	2.56		4.04			5.05			5.44
Middlesex........	7.33																		5.09			
Bound Brook.....	7.38	7.31		8.35		9.02		10.02	11.04	12.02	1.02		2.04	3.02		4.11			5.13			5.50
Manville-Finderne...	7.46															4.15						
Somerville........	7.52			8.41		9.07		10.07	11.11	12.07	1.07		2.11	3.07		4.19			5.21			5.56
Raritan...........	7.56			8.45		9.09		10.09	11.15	12.09	1.09		2.16	3.09		4.22			5.25			5.59
North Branch.....													2.22									
White House.....		Stops at Calco 7.40 a.m.											2.30									
Lebanon..........													2.37									
Annandale........													2.43									
High Bridge......													2.52									
Glen Gardner.....													2.58									
Hampton......Arrive													3.04									

RDC—De Luxe Air Conditioned Rail Diesel Cars (Budd).
†—Leaving or arriving time of connecting train, change at Elizabethport.
‡—Leaving or arriving time of connecting train, change at Elizabethport and Elizabeth.
① Arrives Elizabethport 7.43 A.M.
RDC—De Luxe Air Conditioned Rail Diesel Cars (Budd).
a—Stops on notice to take passengers.
§—Leaving or arriving time of connecting train, change at Elizabethport.
c—Leaving time of connecting train change at E. Ferry St. and Elizabethport.

A distinctive feature of Elizabeth station is its clock tower with its four spires and locomotive weather vane.

Reading lines "Wall Street" a competitor of the Pennsy on the Philly to New York run dashes under its rival at Elizabeth with FP-7 #902 leading the way.
(W.J. Brennan)

Northbound Pennsylvania RR express passes over a stationary Jersey Central eastbound freight at Elizabeth station. This freight is waiting for a yard track at E-Port.

Train #905 the 5:33 PM out of Jersey City bound for Plainfield pauses at Elizabeth for the last time. The Aldene plan takes effect at midnight.

An RS-3 gets under way under its characteristic plume of black diesel oil exhaust with train #1413 the Saturday only 11:12 AM Raritan Clocker.

With trainmaster #2408 in notch 8 train #423 passes Elizabeth station for the last time. It's the 5:22 PM out of Jersey City for Raritan, first stop Fanwood-Scotch Plains.

On February 19, 1966 the 3:12 PM Raritan Clocker departs Elizabeth down the boulevard where B&O's finest varnish once trod.

Bright and shiny like a new silver coin, eastbound Budd RDC set at the same location in 1963.

Trainmaster 2404 passes one of the few remaining milepost markers. It's telling passing trains that they are 12 miles from Jersey City or 78 miles from Reading Terminal Philadelphia. This milepost was located a half mile west of Elizabeth station.

MONDAYS to FRIDAYS incl. except Nov. 8, 24, Dec. 26, Jan. 2, Feb. 22								MONDAYS to FRIDAYS incl. except Nov. 8, 24, Dec. 26, Jan. 2, Feb. 22									
Eastern Standard Time EASTBOUND	3314	RDC 418	RDC 420	104	3316	RDC 422	RDC 424	4002	426	RDC 428	192	1002	430	1004	432	3322	444	616	620
Leave	AM	AM	AM	AM	AM	PM	PM	PM	PM	PM	PM	PM	PM	PM	PM	PM	PM	PM	PM
Hampton		"NEW YORK CLOCKER"	"NEW YORK CLOCKER"	10.35	"NEW YORK CLOCKER"	"NEW YORK CLOCKER"	"NEW YORK CLOCKER"	"NEW YORK CLOCKER"		"NEW YORK CLOCKER"	3.14		"NEW YORK CLOCKER"		Stops at Calco 4.46 p.m.		Stops at Calco 5.18 p.m.	
Glen Gardner				10.38														
High Bridge				10.45							3.23							
Annandale				10.49														
Lebanon				10.54							3.29							
White House				11.00							3.35							
North Branch				11.08														
Raritan		9.14	10.14	11.14		12.14	1.14		2.14	3.14	3.48		4.14		4.23		5.05	
Somerville		9.17	10.17	11.17		12.17	1.17		2.17	3.17	3.51		4.17		4.27		5.09	
Manville-Finderne															4.40		5.15	
Bound Brook		9.23	10.23	11.23		12.23	1.23		2.23	3.23	3.57		4.23		4.49	5Ⓣ21	5.23	6.23
Middlesex																	5.29	
Dunellen		9.29	10.29	11.29		12.29	1.29		2.29	3.29	4.04		4.29		4.55	5.33	5.29	6.29
Clinton Ave., Plfd.															4.57	5.35		
Grant Ave., Plfd.																5.38		
Plainwood-No. Plfd.		9.34	10.34	11.34		12.34	1.34		2.34	3.34	4.10		4.34		5.02	5.48	5.34	6.34
Netherwood-Plfd.															5.04	5.51		
Fanwood-Scotch Pls.																5.54		
Westfield		9.41	10.41	11.41		12.41	1.41		2.41	3.41	4.17		4.41		5.10	6.00	5.41	6.41
Garwood											4.20				5.13			
Cranford		9.45	10.45	11.45		12.45	1.45		2.45	3.45	4.23		4.45		5.16		5.45	6.45
Roselle-Roselle Pk.		9.50	10.50	11.50		12.50	1.50		2.50	3.50	4.28		4.50		5.20		5.50	6.50
Lorraine															5.23			
Elmora Avenue													4.53		5.26			
Elizabeth		9.55	10.55	11.55		12.55	1.55		2.55	3.55	4.34		4.56		5.29		5.55	6.55
Spring Street															5.32			
Elizabethport	9.57	9.59	10.59	11.59	12.25	12.59	1.59	2.54	2.59	3.59	4Ⓑ37	4.49	5.00	5.19	5.35	5.50	5.59	6.59
Kearny ‡																		
Newark ‡		10:14		12:43			‡2.14		3:39		5:05				‡6.16		6‡16	7:15
West 8th St. ⎫	10.03	10.05	11.05	12.05	12.31	1.05	2.05	3.00	3.05	4.06	4.45	4.55	5.06	5.25	5.41	5.56	6.05	7.05
East 22nd St. ⎬ Bay-											4.09	4.58		5.28				
East 33rd St. ⎨ onne	3.08	10.08	11.08	12.08			2.09			4.12	5.00	5.10	5.30				6.09	
East 45th St. ⎭										4.15			5.32					
Greenville									3.12	4.19		5.04		5.35			6.13	
Van Nostrand Pl.														5.37				
Communipaw																		
Jersey City Term.	10.13	10.17	11.17	12.17	12.41	1.15	2.20	3.09	3.18	4.25	4.55	5.10	5.18	5.42	5.51	6.06	6.19	7.15
New York Liberty-Cor'dt St. Arrive	10.26	10.30	11.30	12.30	12.53	1.27	2.32	3.22	3.30	4.40	5.07	5.23	5.30	5.53	6.05	6.20	6.32	7.27
	AM	AM	AM	PM	PM	PM	PM	PM	PM	PM	PM	PM	PM	PM	PM	PM	PM	PM

RDC—De Luxe Air-Conditioned Rail Diesel Cars (Budd).
‡—Leaving or arriving time of connecting train, change at Elizabethport.

RDC—De Luxe Air-Conditioned Rail Diesel Cars (Budd).
‡—Leaving or arriving time of connecting train, change at Elizabethport. Ⓣ—Leaves Bound Brook 5.25 P.M. Ⓑ—Leaves Elizabethport 4.39 P.M.

On February 5, 1966 RS-3 1552 has train #1415 in tow between Elizabeth and Elmora Avenue.

2:12 PM Raritan Clocker, normally an RDC, passing Elmora Avenue with #1511 in command. Note the fencing designed to prevent jaywalking commuters from becoming a news item.

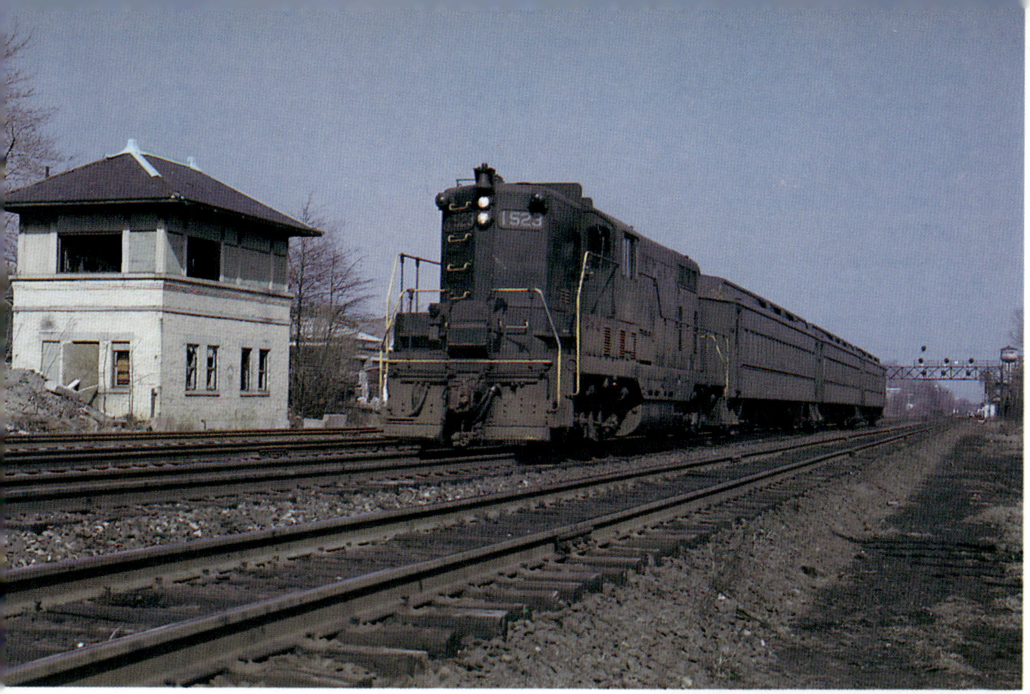

#1523 running against traffic passes abandoned Elmor Tower. In the days of steam westbound freights got pushers here for the grade to Cranford.

Saturday locomotive redistribution gives this westbound at Roselle Park plenty of horses. RS-3 #1555 leads trainmaster #2406 on a short 3 car consist.

NEW YORK TO PHILLIPSBURG, EASTON, BETHLEHEM, ALLENTOWN, READING, LEBANON, HARRISBURG

EASTERN STANDARD TIME		MONDAYS TO FRIDAYS, Incl. except Nov. 3, 26, Dec. 25, Jan. 1, Feb. 22			SATURDAYS and Nov. 3 ONLY			SUNDAYS & Nov. 26, Dec. 25, Jan. 1 ONLY	Feb.22 ONLY
WESTBOUND STATIONS	Miles			"QUEEN OF THE VALLEY"			"QUEEN OF THE VALLEY"	"QUEEN OF THE VALLEY"	"QUEEN OF THE VALLEY"
		101	107	199	1101	1107	1199	2199	2199
		AM	PM	PM	AM	PM	PM	PM	PM
New York Liberty-Cortlandt St. ...... Lv.	.0	3.00	1 00	5.37	3.00	1.00	5.00	5 00	5.00
Jersey City Terminal .... "	1.0	3.30	1.12	5.48	3.30	1 12	5.12	5.12	5.12
West 8th St., Bayonne ...... "	7.6	3.54	1.22	ⓒ5.20	3.54	1.22	5.22	5.22	5.22
Newark (Broad St.) .... "	....	....	x1.10	ⓒ5.11	...	x1.10	x5 10	x5.05	x5.05
Elizabethport .... "	10.6	4.01	1 28	ⓒ5.27	4.01	1.28	5.28	5.28	5 28
Elizabeth .... "	12.5	4.14	1 32	a5§34	4.14	1.32	5.32	5.32	5.32
Roselle-Roselle Park .... "	15.0	4.23	1 36	§5.18	4.24	1.36	5.36	5.36	5.36
Cranford .... "	17.2	4.33	1 40	§5.23	4 32	1.40	5.40	5.40	5.40
Westfield .... "	19.5	4.45	1 44	§5.28	4.45	1.44	5.44	5.44	5.44
Plainfield-North Plainfield ... "	24.0	5.10	1 51	§5.53	5 10	1.51	5.51	5.51	5.51
Bound Brook .... "	31.2	5.34	2 04	6.19	5 34	2.04	6.04	6.04	6.04
Somerville .... "	35.6	6.06	2.11	6.25	6 05	2.11	6.11	6.11	6.11
Raritan .... "	36.8	6.11	2.16	6.28	6.10	2.15	6.15	6 15	6.15
North Branch .... "	40.3	6.18	2.22	6.34	6.16	2.21	6.21	6.20	6.20
White House .... "	45.2	6.28	2.30	6.41	6.28	2.29	6.27	6.25	6.25
Lebanon .... "	49.2	6.36	2.37	6.46	6.35	2.36	6.32	6.30	6.30
Annandale .... "	51.4	6.43	2.43	6.51	6.45	2.42	6.37	6.35	6.35
High Bridge .... "	53.2	6.53	2.52	6.56	6.53	2.47	6.41	6.39	6.39
Glen Gardner .... "	56.1	7.01	2.58	7.01	7.02	2.53	6.46	6.44	6.44
Hampton .... "	57.6	7.08	3.04	7.05	7.07	2.58	6.50	6.48	6.48
Ludlow-Asbury .... "	61.0	7.16	3.10	....	7.13	3.04	......	....	......
Bloomsbury .... "	65.7	7.25	3 17	....	7.20	3.11	......	....	......
Phillipsburg .... "	73.1	7.36	3 28	7.25	7.30	3.20	7.10	7.06	7.06
Easton .... "	73.8	7.47	3.37	7.30	7.40	3.28	7.15	7.09	7.09
Bethlehem .... "	85.3	8.10	3.58	7.51	8.03	3.49	7.35	7.26	7.26
Allentown .... Ar.	90.3	8.20	4.08	8.01	8.13	3.59	7.45	7.36	7.36
Allentown (Rdg. Sys.) ..... Lv.	90.3	....	......	0.25	....	......	8.25	8.44	8.25
Reading .... Ar.	126.1	....	......	9.15	....	......	9.15	9.30	9.15
Pottsville .... "	160.8	....	......	....	....	......	......	Ø11.33	......
Wernersville .... "	134.7	....	......	b9.45	....	......	b9.45	b9.47	b9.45
Lebanon .... "	153.8	....	......	10.18	....	......	10.18	10.14	10.18
Hershey .... "	166.8	....	......	10.37	....	......	10.37	10.30	10.37
Harrisburg .... "	179.5	....	....	10.55	..	......	10.55	10.50	10.55
		AM	PM	PM	AM	PM	PM	PM	PM

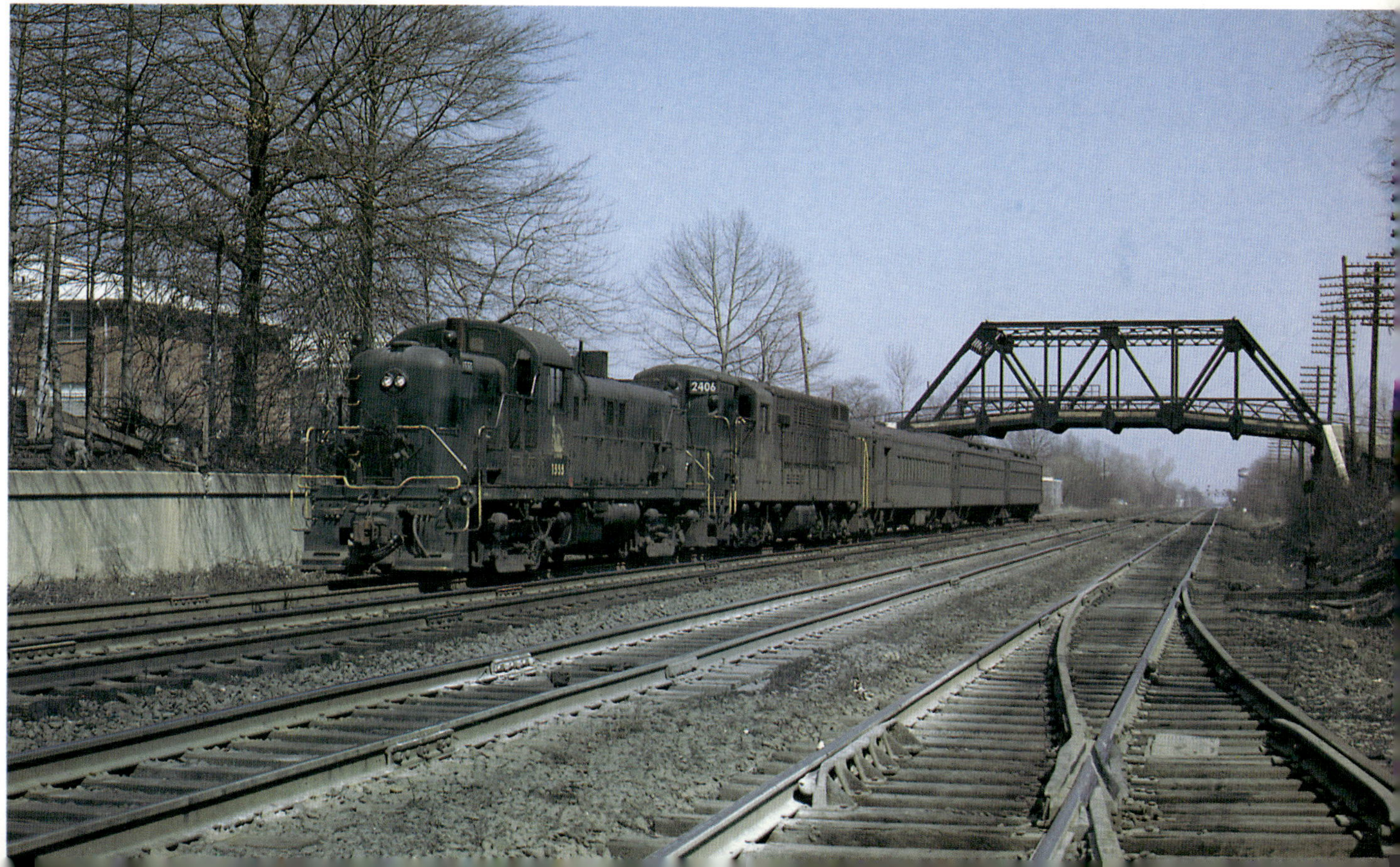

Lengthening shadows act as a final curtain for the last passing of the "Wall Street" led by FP-7 #900 at Roselle Park. Train #905 the 5:33 PM out of Jersey City led by trainmaster #2402 makes its last call at the station.

Train #1419 nears Aldene in an earler, happier winter scene.

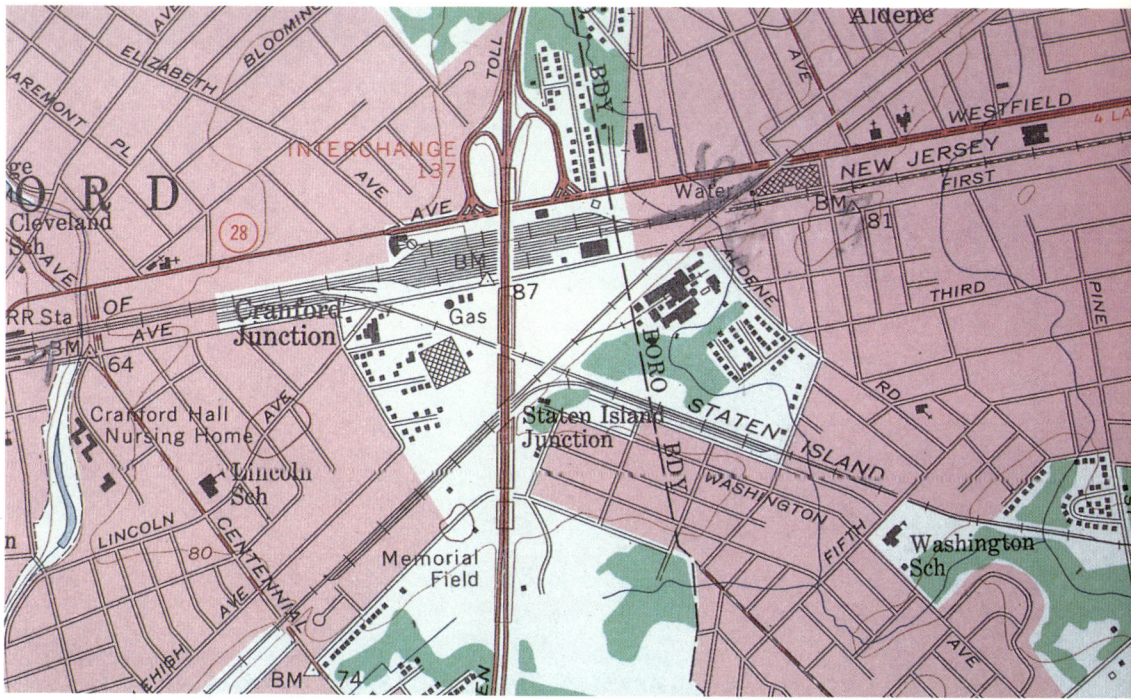

The Lehigh Valley railroad running from the upper right to the lower left crosses on a trestle the Jersey Central running from right to left. The only physical connection between them is at Staten Island Jct. The Aldene plan called for a ramp to be built between both railroads at the trestle located east of Cranford yard.

Train #415 led by GP-7 #1528 passes Aldene, visible on the left is the new ramp that connects the Jersey Central to the Lehigh Valley RR. This ramp gives access to Penn Station Newark and across platform transfers to PATH trains and Pennsylvania RR trains. This made it possible to close Jersey City Terminal and bring to an end the costly ferry service, its existence made necessary because it was the only terminal without a PATH connection to Manhattan.

#2411 passes another vintage mile post at Aldene, it marks the spot as 15 miles from Jersey City or seventy-five miles from Philadelphia. The cribbing on the right marks the upcoming major change in the history of the Central Railroad of New Jersey.

ALDENE PLAN
Commuter Report

   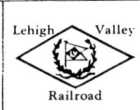 

Issued by the New Jersey Department of Transportation

No. 2   Fe   )67

This is the second of a series of continuing reports to commuters and the public in the North Jersey area on the progress of the State of New Jersey's Aldene Plan for improved rail passenger service.

ALDENE PLAN FARES APPROVED

Public hearings were held by the State on November 18th and December 5th at which details of the proposed fares were outlined and comments received from the public. A decision announced by the Department of Transportation on January 19th granted the fare requests of the railroads.

The Central Railroad Company of New Jersey had applied to the State for permission to reduce its Newark fares in line with the shorter mileage over the Aldene route. For example, a commuter from Westfield will pay $19.45 for a standard monthly ticket to Newark compared with the present fare of $22.90. Plans were revealed for the sale of joint tickets good for travel over the Central main line and the Pennsylvania to Penn Station, New York, at fares lower than a combination of the regular fares of the two railroads. This new ticket will cost the Westfield commuter $36.45 per month.

The Pennsylvania had asked for authorization to eliminate its Penn Station, New York, supplemental tickets and to sell commutation tickets to Penn Station at costs which reflect what most passengers to that destination are actually paying now.

Evidence produced at the hearings showed that the proposed fares would result in a substantial increase in travel costs for Pennsylvania Railroad commuters destined to Jersey City. To prevent undue hardship on these people, the decision by the State requires the Pennsylvania to enter into an agreement with the Public Service Coordinated Transport Company to establish joint rail-bus tickets which will enable Jersey City intrastate passengers to have a choice between the faster all-rail service or a cheaper rail-bus combination. A similar arrangement will be made effective for Jersey City passengers of the Central.

PATH ANNOUNCES LOWER FARES

PATH has announced that when the Aldene Plan begins, the present single trip fares will be reduced from 40¢ to 30¢, which is the interstate standard fare on all other parts of the system. This action will simplify the PATH fare structure and permit an easy transition to a token-turnstile system for Newark travel. The Newark-Journal Square fare will be reduced from 35¢ to 30¢ and the Newark-Harrison fare will remain at 15¢. Turnstiles and new PATH token change booths are now being installed at Pennsylvania Station, Newa where passengers in most cases will be able to transfer direct to PATH trains across the platform from their incoming trains. Automatic token vending machines also will be installed at Newark.

This project is supported in part by Federal funds provided under the Urban Mass Transportation Act of 1964.

ALDENE PLAN
RESTRICTED MONTHLY COMMUTATION FARES
FROM TYPICAL STATIONS

| | NEWARK | | JERSEY CITY | | | NEW YORK | | | |
| | | | | | | LIBERTY ST/HUD. TERM. | | PENN STATION | |
	PRESENT	NEW	PRESENT	NEW(a)	NEW(b)	PRESENT	NEW(b)	PRESENT	NEW
CNJ MAIN LINE									
Roselle Park	$19.45	$14.35	$27.75(c)	$21.70	$26.95	$29.85	$26.95	--	$31.35
Westfield	22.90	19.45	30.65(c)	26.80	32.05	32.75	32.05	--	36.45
Plainfield	25.35	22.90	32.40(c)	30.25	35.50	34.50	35.50	--	39.90
Somerville	29.30	28.00	36.45(c)	35.35	40.60	38.55	40.60	--	45.00
CNJ/PRR SEASHORE									
S. Amboy	$24.85	$24.85	$26.85	$32.20	$37.45	$35.25(d)	$37.45	$39.45(e)	$39.45
Matawan	27.25	27.25	29.05	34.60	39.85	37.45(d)	39.85	41.45(e)	41.45
Red Bank	30.15	30.15	31.55	37.50	42.75	39.95(d)	42.75	43.35(e)	43.35
Asbury Park	33.10	33.10	33.65	40.45	45.70	42.05(d)	45.70	45.20(e)	45.20
PRR MAIN LINE						HUD. TERM.			
Elizabeth	$13.15	$13.15	$19.45	$20.50	$25.75	$23.40	$25.75	$27.60(e)	$27.60
Rahway	18.45	18.45	24.35	25.80	31.05	32.15	31.05	36.35(e)	36.35
New Brunswick	26.10	26.10	29.05	33.45	38.70	37.40	38.70	41.60(e)	41.60
Trenton	36.10	36.10	40.60	43.45	48.70	49.25	48.70	49.25	49.25

(a) Railroad to Newark, Public Service bus beyond
(b) Based on 42 rides per month on PATH @ 30¢ per ride
(c) Includes 42 rides per month local Jersey City bus @ 15¢ per ride
(d) Also applies to Hudson Terminal via PRR-PATH
(e) Based on Hudson Terminal fare plus 42 rides on supplemental tickets

ALDENE PLAN SCHEDULES

Proposed schedules under the Aldene Plan were presented by the Central and Pennsylvania Railroads at public hearings held by the State during late November and early December. Public officials and representatives of several municipalities offered their views at these hearings and the various suggestions for improvement of service are now being reviewed. A decision on the schedules is expected later this month.

PATH has also announced its Aldene Plan service. Trains will be operated out of Newark as frequently as every three minutes during the morning peak; the same service will be available out of Hudson Terminal in lower Manhattan in the evening peak. This compares with a present eight-minute service out of Newark and Hudson Terminal in the daily peak hours. The more frequent service resulting from the improv schedules and additional new cars will enable PATH to carry the increased passenger volume.

Since November, good progress has been made on essential construction work and planning which should permit the start of service by all participants in the Plan on April 30, 1967.

ALDENE WORK IN PROGRESS

CNJ "PUSH-PULL" CAR

A major feature of the Aldene Plan is the rehabilitation by the Central Railroad of New Jersey of 140 passenger coaches. The one shown above is a "push-pull" car. In "push-pull" operations, a car such as this is placed at one end of a train, with a locomotive at the opposite end. With controls in the "push-pull" car, the train can operate in either direction without having to be turned around, thus eliminating time-consuming switching operations. Over 110 CNJ passenger coaches — some "push-pull", some regular coaches — have been modernized so far.

ROSELLE PARK STATION and PLATFORM

The new Roselle Park Station, with its protective canopy and high-level platform, will offer comfort and convenience for CNJ Aldene passengers. The station, shown above, is being constructed by the State of New Jersey. The high-level platform speeds boarding time by eliminating the need for passengers to step up to the train vestibule level. The overhead canopy, fiberglass windscreen panels and enclosed stairwells provide inclement weather protection. Numerous parking spaces will be available as well as a "kiss n' ride" driveway for commuters whose wives drive them to the station.

NEW PATH CARS

The first three of PATH's new 44 air-conditioned transit cars, ordered in connection with the Aldene Plan, are shown above in the South Street Yard, Newark. The new cars supplement the fleet of 162 similar cars placed in PATH service in 1965 and incorporate the same modern features for passenger comfort — well-lighted interiors, comfortable seating arrangements, public address systems, directional signs and tinted windows. These new cars will be in service for commuters travelling on PATH between Newark and Hudson Terminal. When Aldene begins, PATH will operate trains out of Newark every three minutes in the commuting peak periods, instead of the present eight-minute intervals. Off-peak service during the day will be at 10 minute intervals. PATH operates 24 hours a day, seven days a week.

NEW PATH TRACK

As part of the Aldene Plan, a new eastbound track in the Newark-Harrison area is being constructed for PATH (shown above looking east from the Harrison Station). The new track will separate PATH's rapid transit operation from Pennsylvania Railroad freight tracks. In addition, improvements to PATH's signal and power systems are being made. PATH track running parallel with the Passaic River in Kearny is being raised to prevent disruptions in service when heavy rains cause the river to overflow. After Aldene begins, PATH will assume the entire operation of the line between Newark and Journal Square, now operated under a joint service arrangement with PRR.

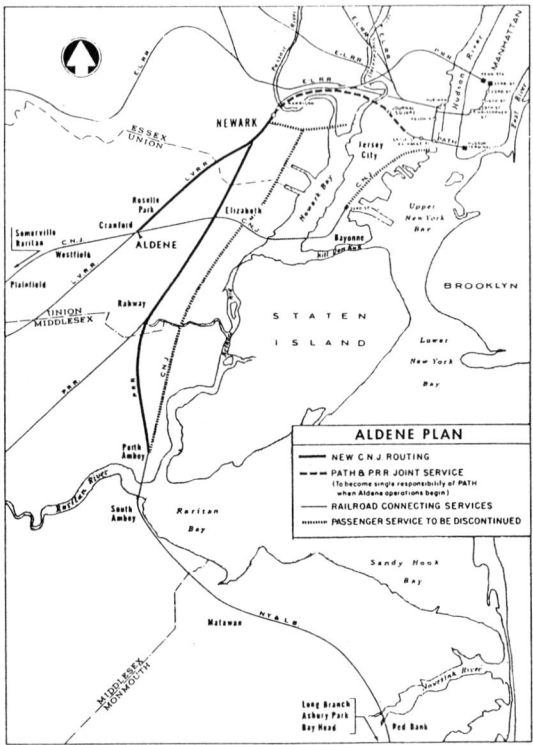

The Aldene Plan was conceived by the State Highway Department's Division of Railroad Transportation as a means of preserving essential railroad passenger service for thousands of north Jersey rail commuters.

The concept involves the rerouting of passenger trains of the Central Railroad Company (CNJ) into Pennsylvania Station, Newark. Mainline trains of the CNJ will switch to Lehigh Valley Railroad (LV) tracks at a point east of Cranford (Aldene Junction) and then to the tracks of the Pennsylvania Railroad (PRR). CNJ shore trains will follow PRR tracks from Perth Amboy. Passengers traveling to New York City will be able to complete their trips by using either the Port Authority Trans-Hudson (PATH) rail rapid transit system to lower and mid-Manhattan or mainline trains of the PRR to Penn Station, New York.

The CNJ also will provide passenger service between Cranford and Bayonne.

The new route will provide direct rail service from the densely-populated corridor centered on Somerville, Plainfield and Westfield into downtown Newark. It will make possible the continuation of CNJ passenger service by reducing operating deficits, and eliminating the deficit ferry service between Jersey City and Liberty Street in lower Manhattan.

To complete this vital program, the State of New Jersey has appropriated $6,1000,000 and has obtained a grant of $3,600,000 from the Federal Government under the 1964 Urban Mass Transportation Act. An additional $15,200,000 is being spent on improvements to the PATH system, $5,100,000 of which represents a Federal grant.